Six Little Cooks, Or, Aunt Jane's Cooking Class

"EACH EGG WAS TO BE BROKEN BY ITSELF IN A CUP FIRST, BEFORE GOING TO JOIN ITS COMPANIONS IN THE DISH."—PAGE 11.

SIX

LITTLE COOKS;

OR

AUNT JANE'S

COOKING CLASS.

CHICAGO:
JANSEN, McCLURG & CO.
1877.

COPYRIGHT.
JANSEN, McCLURG & CO.
A. D. 1877.

STEREOTYPED AND PRINTED
BY THE
CHICAGO LEGAL NEWS CO.

SIX LITTLE COOKS;

OR,

AUNT JANE'S COOKING CLASS.

FIRST DAY.

"Oh, Aunt Jane," said Grace, looking up quickly from the story-book she was reading, "I wish you would teach us all how to cook!"

But here am I, the author, plunging at once into the middle of my story without a word of explanation, not even a preface. Of course, no one can understand anything about it unless I go back a little, and tell you how it began.

Aunt Jane had come to make a visit to Mrs. Vernon, Grace's mother, and had brought her own little girl, Amy, to spend the vacation. Next door lived Edith Lane, a very intimate friend of both the girls, and just across the street, Rose and Jessie Carroll, Grace's cousins; and these five, with little Mabel Vernon, made a happy company who were almost always together. Mabel was just nine years old, and the others were from ten to twelve, so there was not difference enough in their ages to prevent their being the best of playmates.

Well—as I began to say, Grace was reading about a wonderful little girl who made such remarkable things in the way of cakes and puddings, that our young person was seized with a desire to do likewise without delay. Aunt Jane was the kindest of aunts and the best of cooks, and Grace knew that if she would take the trouble to teach them, they would be well taught.

"I should like that of all things," said she, in answer to Grace's exclamation, "provided your mother consents."

"Oh, she'd be perfectly delighted," cried Grace; "she often says she wishes she had time to teach us herself."

"Very well, then; run and ask her if we may begin this afternoon."

"And c.n't Rose and Jessie and Edith come too?" inquired Grace eagerly. "They all want to learn, just as much as I do."

"Not quite so fast," said Aunt Jane, smiling. "Suppose we begin with those in the house first, and if it works well we can invite the others afterwards."

So Grace ran off to get her mother's answer, tripping over a footstool as she went, banging her head against the edge of the door in her haste to get round it, and catching her sleeve in a corner of the banisters. She always began everything with the same wild enthusiasm, but was somewhat apt to grow weary of the new employment before she had thoroughly tried it.

" Yes, of course," she called out, while she was still on her way down stairs, " mamma says you couldn't do her a greater favor. May we begin now?"

"I think we will wait until after dinner," said her aunt. "Then we shall not be interrupted, nor be in Rhoda's way."

As it was summer, the family dined in the middle of the day, and as soon as propriety would allow, the impatient children announced that they were ready.

" But I think I see the need of some preparations first," said Aunt Jane.

" Washing our hands? Oh, Aunty, we all washed them just the last thing before dinner!"

"And you ate your breakfast yesterday, but that didn't prevent your wanting it again this morning! The very last thing a neat cook does before she goes to work is to wash her hands and clean her nails carefully; and, not to disturb Rhoda more than is necessary, you may do it in your own rooms. But I see something else that is wanted —or rather, I *don't* see it, because it isn't here!"

"Oh, I know," said Mabel. "Aprons!"

"But we haven't any," said Grace. "I never wear aprons with my calico dresses."

"But an apron is almost as necessary for cooking—for neat cooking, I mean,—as a pair of hands. I have one in my trunk that will do for Amy, and you can borrow a couple more from your mother. To-morrow I'll get some gingham and make you each one; that is, if you should ever care to try it again."

"Oh, Aunty!" and "Oh, mamma!" broke in chorus from three pairs of rosy lips.

"Well—we shall see. And now there is one thing more I should like to have you do. Bring a little blank book, in which you can write down the recipes we try, and if any of them should prove not to be good, we'll cross them off without mercy."

The book was quickly brought, and Grace wrote down from her aunt's dictation, as follows:

No. 1.—SUSAN'S CAKE.

Three cups flour, two of sugar, two-thirds of a cup of butter, one cup of sour milk, three eggs, one teaspoonful soda, two of cream tartar. Two cups seeded raisins, or one of well-washed currants, added, makes a delicious fruit cake.

No. 2.—BAKED CUSTARD.

One quart milk, six eggs—omitting two whites—(five will do when they are scarce, and omit one white)—six tablespoonfuls granulated sugar, flavoring to taste. Bake in small cups.

No. 3.—POPOVERS.

One cup flour, one of milk, one egg, a piece of butter the size of a walnut, a pinch of salt. Bake in gem pans.

"What a funny name, Aunty—popovers!" exclaimed Mabel, when Grace had finished writing.

"Perhaps you call them muffins here," replied her aunt, "but I like the old-fashioned name. At all events, I know they are very good."

"Why do you call it Susan's cake, Aunt Jane?" asked Grace.

"Because our old German cook, Susan, showed me how

to make it," said Mrs. King (by the way, Mrs. King was Aunt Jane's company name,) "and I never happened to meet with it anywhere else."

"What next, Aunty?"

"That will be enough for to-day. We will try all those, and if they do well you shall have some more next time. Now let us go down to the kitchen."

Rhoda, the black cook, looked with some suspicion on the small army invading her precincts, but she knew by experience that the children were well-behaved and respectful, never giving unnecessary trouble or returning saucy answers if checked; so she made up her mind to bear the infliction with a good grace.

"You shall make the cake, Grace, and Amy the custard," said Aunt Jane. " Mabel may help you with these, now, and she and I will come again, just before tea, and attend to the popovers. Now begin by collecting what is named in your recipes."

Every thing was soon neatly arranged on the large kitchen table, and Aunt Jane began her instructions. She told the girls to break the eggs with yolks and whites separate for the cake; together for the custard, and showed them how to do it neatly without mingling the two.

Those for the cake were to be beaten first, so as to use the same dishes for both, and not soil a second set. Each egg was to be broken by itself into a cup first, before going to join its companions in the dish, as a single one carelessly thrown in when not perfectly fresh, might spoil the entire mixture. This is a rule it is never safe for the most skillful cook to neglect.

"But what shall we do with the two extra whites that are left from the custard, Aunty?" asked Mabel.

"Rhoda will save them to clear the coffee with," replied Mrs. King. "But if there were more we could easily use them in our cooking, for many nice things are made with the whites alone."

When the eggs were beaten, one part to a yellow cream and the other to a stiff white froth, the sugar and butter were rubbed together, little by little, with a strong spoon. Then the yolk of egg was added and stirred until the whole was perfectly smooth. The cream tartar was thrown into the flour, ready to be passed through the sieve, and then Aunt Jane told Grace to take a quarter cup of warm water (not boiling) to dissolve her soda in.

"Some people throw the soda directly into the sour milk," said she, "but it is a poor way, and accounts for

the unpleasant little lumps of alkali we sometimes find
in cake and biscuit.   Mabel, while Gracie is putting her
cake together, you may butter and warm the cake-tins,
otherwise she would have to wait and do that first, for
the cake musn't stand a minute longer than is necessary
after the soda is once in."

Then the whites of eggs were stirred in, all but the
liquid remainder which had settled, and which was well
beaten before being added, and the water containing the
soda was carefully poured off into the sour milk, leaving
the sediment in the bottom of the cup.   The milk bubbled
and foamed, as much as to protest against such doings,
and would soon have overrun its bounds altogether, but
that just at the critical moment it was tumbled into
the rest of the mixture, a beautiful cataract of white
foam.

"It's for your own good, you know," said Grace, ad-
dressing it.   "It's to make you sweet."

All else being ready, the flour was now sifted in, Grace
stirring vigorously all the while.   When the whole was
smoothly mixed, the little tins were filled rather less than
half full, and all set into the large dripping-pan to bake.

" Anything so delicate as this might be injured by not

being taken out the moment it was done," said Aunt Jane, " so the best way is to do it all at once; besides which, it saves trouble."

In the meantime, Amy had prepared her custard, except the flavoring. "What kind shall I put in, mamma?" said she.

" Suppose we try some bitter almond to-day," answered her mother. " Nothing can be more delicious to those who like it, and I see your Aunt Nelly does, or she wouldn't have this great bottle of it in the pantry. One teaspoonful will do if it is as strong as it ought to be, and if we find it not enough, we can add more next time. It is always better to put too little of any flavoring or spice than too much."

Another dripping-pan was brought and half filled with boiling water, which was ready in the teakettle, that the China cups might not be burnt. These were then filled to within a quarter of an inch of the top, set into the pan of hot water, and the whole placed in the oven.

" Your recipe doesn't say how long we must bake these things," said Grace.

" There is very little use in giving any exact direction about that," answered her aunt. " Stoves vary so much that half an hour in one means the same as three quarters in another. I think this one will bake the cake in half an hour, and the custard in somewhat less, but we must watch them. There is no absolute rule but experience."

Aunt Jane was right, and everything was done to a turn, just as she predicted. When the cakes were taken out they were placed on the sieve for a short time to cool. A little nutmeg—very little—was grated over the top of each custard, and all were set away in the dark pantry, out of the reach of flies and dust. About three-quarters of an hour before tea-time, Mrs. King showed Mabel, as she had promised, how to make the popovers.

"I think we shall have to double this recipe," said she, "for it makes only twelve, and as we are eight at our table, with the boys, and shall want to leave some for Rhoda and the rest, we'll take two eggs, and so on."

Then Aunt Jane told Mabel that the great point was to have her mixture perfectly smooth and without lumps, which would be done only by adding the milk very slowly to the flour, stirring constantly. The eggs, beaten together without separating yolks and whites, went in last of all. Then half of the little straight-sided tins, buttered first, of course, and warmed, were filled less than half full, and pop they went into the oven. "They ought to bake in fifteen minutes," said Aunt Jane.

And so they did. You ought to have seen those muffins, or popovers, or whatever else you like to call them, when they came out of that oven. How they had risen and over-topped their boundaries, and how they bulged out over the sides, and flowed about in waves of brown crust! Mabel fairly danced with delight, clapping her hands and throwing her arms round Aunt Jane's neck in an ecstasy of gratitude. In the meantime, Rhoda quietly filled the rest of the tins and set them in the oven to be ready when the second installment was called for. The three cooks marched into the supper-room in triumph, and when the excellent appetites of the family showed their full appreciation of what was set before them, you have seldom seen a prouder set of girls than ours were after their first day's efforts at cooking.

SECOND DAY.

What do you think was the first question Mrs. King heard the next morning, almost before she had opened her eyes? It was, "Oh, Aunt Jane, are we going to cook again to-day?"

"Cook?" said Aunt Jane, sleepily, "cook what? Oh, yes, I remember. I can tell you better after I have had a cup of coffee. I never know anything before breakfast."

She relented so far, however, as to tell Grace at the table, in order to set her mind at ease, that she thought it would be best to postpone the next lesson until another day, and devote her energies to the making of aprons.

"One apiece will be enough," said she, "for you couldn't very well be in the kitchen on washing and ironing days; so when the apron is soiled it can be made clean in the early part of the week, and you can use it again in the latter part. You may go in and ask Aunt Carroll and Mrs. Lane if they would like to have their little girls join the cooking-club, and then we shall know how many aprons will be needed."

There was not much doubt about the answer, but to make matters sure, all those invited came instantly rushing in, out of breath, to say that their mammas were very much obliged and when should they come and what should they bring with them and what kind of cloth would be needed for the aprons and how much? As all this was without a pause, of course the truthful historian is not allowed to introduce any punctuation.

"Oh, I'll attend to all that," said Aunt Jane, as soon as she could get in a word. "The aprons shall be my present to the club. I'll go down town now and get the materials, and if you like, we'll have a sewing-bee afterwards, and you can help make them up. Many hands make light work, you know."

Agreed to on all sides.

Three pretty ginghams were chosen, two of each color, so that they could easily be distinguished; Mrs. King cut them out and ran them up on the sewing-machine, and the children finished them off under her direction. Good, serviceable aprons they were, high in the neck and coming down to the very bottom of the dress—loose and

2

easy, yet not clumsy. They had sleeves gathered into a wristband and buttoned at the wrist, so that in summer they could be worn without a dress, if desirable, while in winter they would cover a close sleeve. When the little circle were waiting for their work, Aunt Jane said:

"While I am cutting out I'll tell you something, if you like, about what happened to me in one of my experiments in cooking when I was about Grace's age."

Chorus of voices, " Oh, do, do!"

"We lived in the country then, and my mother had a large family of young children, and was so burdened with cares that life was very hard for her. Half the time we could not get any servant, and it was only as a great favor that a woman would come now and then to help with the washing. As I was the oldest daughter, I was brought up to think it my business to do what I could to help along, and being strong and quite intelligent for my age, I really was of great use. One summer we had an unusually fine crop of tomatoes in the garden, (tomatoes were not as common then as they are now, and were considered a great treat,) and my overworked mother was lamenting that she could not make up a quantity of catsup, which my father was very fond of.

"'Let me do it, mamma,' I cried; 'I know I could if you would just show me how.'

"As there was nothing complicated about the recipe, my mother consented, and I had a whole day set apart for the business. First, I was obliged to go and gather the tomatoes, as no one else had time for it; and I was so determined to do myself credit that I brought in one basketful after another until I had a wash-tub full. After that, they had to be looked over and cut up, and a variety of things put with them,—I don't remember exactly what, but it was a very troublesome recipe. The end was that I had a large wash-boiler filled with the rich red mass, and it was set on the stove to boil. If I were doing the same thing now, I should divide the quantity into at least four parts and heat them in separate vessels; but I did not know what poor economy of time and trouble it is to cook too much of anything at once."

"You hadn't any Aunt Jane to teach you," observed Jessie.

"No; and my mother, who had the best practical good sense of any woman I ever saw, was in another part of the house taking care of a sick baby, and had to leave me to my own devices. As my catsup would of course take a long time even to ' come to a boil,' as it is called, there was no use in my standing in the hot kitchen watching it all the time, so I left a good fire under it and took my book out into the wood-shed, where it was cooler. I am sorry to be obliged to confess that at that time I was a regular bookworm, which I have since discovered to mean a person who selfishly pursues her own pleasure in reading, generally to the neglect of plain duties which are staring her in the face, if she would only raise her eyes to see them."

" Oh, I know whom you mean, Aunt Jane," interrupted Grace, " just as well as if you said the name, though you *are* looking the other way so carefully!"

" I made no personal remarks, Gracie; one bookworm is very much like another, as far as my observation goes. But, as I was saying, I took my book, which happened to be a delightful new story, (and story-books were very scarce with me in those days), and was soon absorbed in it. I don't know how long I read, but at last I thought of my tomatoes, and with the thought, or perhaps suggesting it, came a most powerful odor from the kitchen, which I knew betokened no good. Then I ran in fast enough, and there was my great boiler full of tomatoes—"

"Burnt, Aunt Jane?" said Rose.

"The lower layer burned almost to a crisp, and the whole mass so penetrated through and through with the offensive taste, that there was nothing to be done but lift off the boiler and turn the whole contents into the swill-pail! You may imagine the misery and mortification of that moment. My mother arrived on the scene at the same time, and I expected the reproaches I deserved; but she, remembering my patient toil through the early part of the day, and my good intentions, kindly tried to laugh it off, knowing that the consciousness of my failure would be punishment enough. 'I have heard of "cooking by the book,"' said she, 'but I never saw it done exactly in that way before.'

"We had no tomato catsup that year."

"Oh, Aunt Jane, that was too bad!" exclaimed the chorus. "Do you think we shall ever do anything like that?"

"Nothing quite so bad, I hope, but I wouldn't advise you ever to take a very interesting book into the kitchen with you. Time flies so fast when we are reading, that it isn't safe to trust ourselves."

"What am I going to make first, Mrs. King?" inquired Edith. "And I, and I?" chimed in several other voices.

"I will give you some recipes to write down in your book," said Aunt Jane, "and then we can choose from among them. And as I don't think seven of us at once would be very welcome in the kitchen, I propose that we should divide the club into two parts, only half of them to work at one time."

Chorus of groans, "Oh, that won't be half so nice!"

"I think it will be nicer," said Mrs. King. "If there are so many of us we shall only get in each other's way, and then think of the quantity of dishes we should use!"

So it was settled that Rose, Edith and Grace should be the performers for the next afternoon, and in order that all might be quite ready, Mrs. King gave them the following recipes, which they copied into their books:

No. 4—K. K.'s WINE JELLY.

Dissolve one ounce of Cox's sparkling gelatine in a pint of cold water; then pour over it a quart of boiling water; add the grated rind of one lemon and the juice of three, half a pint of Sherry wine, a pinch of ground cinnamon, and sugar to taste. One-and-a-half pounds (or pints) of sugar will be enough for most palates.

No. 5—Chocolate Cake.

One cup butter, two of sugar, three and a half of flour, one scant cup sweet milk, five eggs, omitting two whites, one teaspoonful cream tartar, one-half do. soda, one do. extract vanilla.

Meringue for the same. Beat the whites of the two eggs very light with one and a half cups powdered sugar; six tablespoonfuls grated chocolate, two teaspoonfuls vanilla. Put the meringue on while the cake is hot, and leave it in the pan to cool.

"I don't see how any one can judge of what a 'cup-full' is, Aunt Jane," said Rose, "cups are of such different sizes. Papa's coffee-cup is a perfect monster, and mamma's tea-cup is a mite, small enough for a fairy."

"Kitchen cups are not apt to vary much in size," replied Aunt Jane, "and those are what are taken as a measure. If there is a great difference, we should choose one of a medium size. Then, you must remember, that when there are several things measured in cups, they will be proportioned to one another; so if you find after one experiment that your cake has not enough eggs in proportion to the other ingredients, you will know that your cups are too large; if the egg is too predominating, it will be because the cups are too small; so you will soon learn the happy medium."

"Besides," said Edith, "I suppose every little girl will have some grown person to show her about these things the first time, and then, after that she can remember. Won't you give us some more receipts, Mrs. King?"

"Here they are," said Aunt Jane. "The next is"

No. 6—SPONGE CAKE.

Ten eggs, three cups flour, three of sugar, juice and rind of one lemon, half a tea-cupful cold water. Beat the eggs separately, then add sugar and lemon to the yolks, then the whites, and lastly, sift in the flour. A tea-spoonful of baking-powder, dissolved in half a cup of cold water, is thought by many to be an improvement.

No. 7—BOILED CUSTARD.

One quart milk, six eggs, two teaspoonfuls vanilla extract; sweeten to taste.

"That's another thing I am sure would drive me distracted," said Grace. "How can you know that sugar enough for your taste would be enough for anybody else's?"

"Only by practice, my dear," answered her aunt. "The amount of sugar some people require in custards and sauces is really sickish to others, and each cook must consult the wishes of her own family. But now let us go on to"

.No. 8—MOCK SPONGE CAKE.

Six eggs, beaten one minute, whites and yolks together, three cups sugar, beaten with the eggs for five minutes, one cup cold water, three teaspoonfuls baking powder, rind and juice of one lemon, nearly three cups flour.

No. 9—TIPSY-CAKE.

Take either kind of sponge-cake, cut it into oblong pieces, stick it full of blanched almonds cut into slices, pour over it as much wine as it will absorb, lay it in a glass bowl (if you have one), and pour over it the boiled custard for which the receipt is given above.

No. 10—SOFT CUSTARD.

One quart milk, one tablespoonful corn-starch, two teaspoonfuls vanilla, five ounces sugar, three eggs, a pinch salt.

"There's an exact amount of sugar," observed Edith.

"That is taken from Mrs. Miller's receipt-book," said Aunt Jane, "and she is always exact about everything. But I think these will 'do for to-day, and you may come in to-morrow, as soon as Rhoda's dinner dishes are out of the way."

At the appointed time our three little women, with Aunt Jane at their head, proceeded to the kitchen, in the newest of aprons, the cleanest of hands and the gayest of spirits.

"I think it would be a good plan to make something to-day in the way of a dessert," said Mrs. King; "that will be nice to have cold for dinner to-morrow."

"Oh, do let us make tipsy-cake," said Grace. "I *love* tipsy-cake! Don't you, Aunt Jane?"

"I generally save my love for my friends," replied her aunt, laughing, "but I like tipsy-cake very much. You may make the custard, Grace, and Rosy the cake; and as your mamma said she wanted some jelly to send to some poor sick women, Edith shall try her hand at that."

"Which kind of sponge-cake shall I make?" asked Rose, "the mock or the other?"

"Either is very good, but I think to-day we will make the simpler kind, as it is only to put in custard. That is a very good way, too, to use sponge or any other kind of light cake that has grown a little dry.   Take one of those yellow dishes to stir the cake in; it is never as well to use tin for any such purpose.   Edith, I had your gelatine put to soak before dinner, or it would not have been ready now.   That is something one must always think of beforehand.   Don't break the whites and yolks separately for the custard, Grace; and set the tea-kettle into the stove, so that the water will be boiling when you need it. That is one thing which should always be ready for use in the kitchen.   One *must* have plenty of hot water."

"What do I want hot water for, Aunt Jane?"

"Oh, didn't I tell you?   Any thing in which milk and flour or milk and eggs are to be boiled together, has to be very carefully treated to prevent its getting lumpy.   We always set the vessel in which custard is to be made, into another containing boiling water; or, what is still better, have one that will fit into the top of the other, and so heat it by the steam."

"How long shall I beat the eggs?" asked Grace.

"I think you have whipped them long enough— they don't require much beating for custard.   Let me see how they look.   If there is the least suspicion of an 'eye' in them they must be strained; but these seem all right. Now stir in the sugar and vanilla, and then pour slowly into the warm milk, and keep stirring until it is as thick as good rich cream. How I wish my garden were near enough for me to step in and get you a handful of fresh peach leaves!"

"What would you do with them, Aunt Jane?" said Rose.

"I would boil them in the milk first, or rather, not let it actually come to a boil, but just heat them together to bring out the taste of the peach leaves, and then let it cool before stirring in the eggs. I think there is no flavor more delicious."

Then Mrs. King showed Edith how to make her jelly, first rolling the lemons on the table, so as to break up the hard inner walls and squeeze out the juice more easily. "You may leave out the cinnamon," she said; "as the jelly is for sick people, they might not relish the taste. When it is ready, you must dip the flannel bag you are going to strain it through into hot water and wring it out as dry as possible, so that the jelly may run through easily."

"Shan't I squeeze the jelly-bag a little?" asked Edith,

when the operation was about half over "It seems to run through so slowly."

"Not unless you want the jelly to be thick and muddy-looking. You mustn't even shake it. Leave it in a warm place, and all will run through that ought to. In the meantime, if you want something to do, you may blanch the almonds for the tipsy-cake."

Mrs. King then showed her how to do this, by putting the shelled nuts into boiling water until the wrinkled brown skin would rub off easily, after which it was easy to cut them into thin slips ready to garnish the cake.

The jelly ran through at last, though Edith firmly believed it never would, and was beautifully clear. Then it was poured into several small moulds and set away in the ice-box, as the weather was warm. In winter, the pantry would have done very well. The sponge-cake looked light and spongy, and the custard was as smooth as fresh cream, but Aunt Jane said it would be better to leave them separate until just before dinner, and then dip the cake in wine and pour the custard over it, as otherwise it might become too soft and lose its shape. Need I say that the dessert was excellent, and that the sick people enjoyed their jelly?

THIRD DAY.

"To-day it is the little ones' turn," said Aunt Jane the next morning. "What nice things can we contrive for them to do?"

"Something easy, please," said Mabel, who was a timid little thing, and hadn't much confidence in herself.

"Something nice," said Jessie, who was a year older and twice as ambitious. "Just as good as what the big girls make." (The big girls, by the way, were of the venerable ages of eleven and twelve.)

"Something that my mamma chooses," said Amy, "and then it will be sure to be good."

"I shall try to please you all," said Aunt Jane, patting her little daughter's soft cheek. "Amy can make some Daisy cake for tea, Jessie shall try her hand at a cherry-pudding for dinner, and Mabel may undertake the sauce. Now you may write down the recipes."

No. 11—CHERRY PUDDING.

Two cups milk, one tablespoon butter, two eggs, two

teaspoonfuls cream tartar, one of soda, three light pints flour, or enough to make a stiff batter, one quart cherries, measured after stemming.   Boil or steam two hours.

—— No. 12—Berry Pudding.

The same recipe as for No. 11, substituting berries for cherries.

No. 13—Daisy's Cake.

Three eggs, half a pint sugar, half a pint flour, two tablespoonfuls sweet milk, one teaspoonful baking powder, rind and juice of one lemon.

No. 14—Creamy Pudding-Sauce.

Half a pound brown sugar, a quarter of a pound butter, four tablespoonfuls sweet cream, juice and rind of one lemon.

"First we will attend to the pudding, as that takes the longest to cook," said Aunt Jane. "Amy, you may beat the eggs and grate and squeeze the lemon for your cake; Mabel may pick the cherries off their stems, and see that every one is perfectly clean—no scrap of a leaf or anything else sticking to it—and Jessie can begin upon the pudding."

"What is a 'light pint,' Aunt Jane?" said Jessie.

"A pint not pressed down very hard. One of the first things you have to learn is just how to measure flour. It musn't be packed too hard, or your cake will be hard too; it musn't be put in too lightly, or the cake will fall and be heavy and 'soggy.' It must be pressed down just hard enough, and that you'll soon learn how to do."

"I don't see any half-pint measure here, mamma," said Amy.

"A common tumbler holds half a pint; not one of those that slant in towards the bottom, but one that goes down straight, like this. Now, Jessie, you may warm the butter a little, so that it will stir easily into the milk. We need not be as particular not to melt it as we are in making cake. Dissolve the soda in a quarter of a tea-cup of warm water—not boiling, remember, or you destroy its strength—measure your flour and put the cream tartar into the sieve with it, so that it may be thoroughly mixed."

"Can't you ever use flour without sifting, Aunt Jane?" asked Jessie, who was not fond of taking extra trouble.

"Never, if you want to be sure of having things nice,"

said her aunt. "In the first place, you often find scraps of other things in the flour, like little sticks or straws; and then the sifting makes it much easier to mix with any liquid, and less liable to be lumpy. Now beat the eggs—not very long—and then stir all together, putting the flour in last. Ah! your pints must have been a little too light; that is not quite what is called a stiff batter; we must put in a little more. There, that will do. Now stir it in very thoroughly, putting in the cherries gradually."

"What's that funny-looking thing for, Aunt Jane?" asked Jessie.

"That is called a form, and is to pour the pudding into. In old times, before such things were known, we used either to bake our batter-puddings in the oven, or make them stiff enough to tie in a cloth. This is a great improvement."

The batter was now poured into the form, (which was previously well buttered,) leaving a little room for it to swell in, and the form, after being tightly closed, was plunged into the kettle of boiling water ready to receive it. "Now we can forget all about it for two hours," said Aunt Jane, "except that we must be sure not to let

3

the water boil away so that any part of the form is left uncovered. Now, Amy dear, for your cake."

Amy had the eggs beaten and every thing measured out, so there was nothing to do but put it together, which was a very simple matter, there being no butter. First the sugar and yolks were beaten up, then the lemon was added, then the milk; afterward a little flour (sifted with the baking-powder) and a little white of egg alternately, until all was in.

"This can be baked in one large cake or in the little gem-tins, just as you please, Amy," said her mother. "Which shall it be?"

"Oh, the little ones, please! They look so cunning, and then it seems so much more when there are a good many of them!"

"Very well; you may butter the tins and fill them half full, then put them all into one pan, as we did the first day. Are you almost tired of waiting for your turn, Mabel?"

"Oh, no," said Mabel, "I love to look on and see the girls doing these things."

"We must get out the scales for your 'creamy sauce,' and you can learn how to weigh things. We will take the sugar first, because that will not soil anything. And that reminds me of a suggestion I saw in an excellent receipt-book lately, that there should be paper bags ready to slip sugar and flour and such dry things into after they were weighed and measured, so as to save using so many dishes. I thought it would be a good plan to try it."

" Shall we make some bags, aunty?"

"No, I think we need not do that if Rhoda will save us some of those that are sent from the grocers. They are usually only burnt up. Now take a good large bowl for beating your pudding-sauce in, so that you won't be afraid of spattering anything. You must stir the butter to a cream first with the smallest-sized wooden spoon, then add the sugar, little by little, and afterward the cream, beating them all the while until they are as light as possible. The lemon goes in last. Some people put a little wine, but I think we'll do without that. Now we will just take off the cover of the tea-kettle and set the bowl into it. After a while it will all be melted together into a thick, creamy froth, and then it may be taken off, but it must not be allowed to get cool until it is served. You must ask Rhoda to keep it in a warm place, and then just heat it up the last thing before she sends in the pudding, but not boil it. Pudding sauces should never boil."

"Do just see how Mabel has spelt 'recipe' on the cover of her book!" said Grace, who had just come in and was spying around. "Ressipy-book!"

"That's a very natural mistake," said Aunt Jane kindly, "and it isn't quite polite in you to laugh at her. She spells it as it sounds. When I was a little girl nobody said anything but receipt-books; now that 'recipe' seems to be the fashion, I have adopted it, but I find myself quite as often speaking of 'receipts,' and I think there is something to be said in its favor. However, the main point is to find out whether the dishes made after our recipes are good. Mabel has plenty of time yet to learn how to spell them."

When the pudding came on the table, attended by its foaming sauce, there was a general murmur of approbation; but after everybody had been helped, and had eaten the first spoonful, the murmur changed to many-voiced applause.

"Really remarkably good," said papa; "you don't mean to say that my little Mabel actually made this sauce? Mabel, I see you are destined to be the support of your father's gray hairs.   What shall we do to reward these industrious cooks?"

"I know what I wish you would do," said Grace; "but I'm afraid you won't."

"No harm in telling what it is," said her mother. "Perhaps we will."

"Let us make some candy this afternoon, and ask all the other girls to come in," said Grace, boldly, looking out of the corners of both eyes at once, to see the effect of her proposition.

"I think you might better ask Aunt Jane first if she chooses to spend the afternoon as well as the morning in your instruction."

"Aunt Jane would like the fun as well as any body," observed that obliging relative.

"Then, as this happens to be Rhoda's afternoon out, and you can have the kitchen all to yourselves, I,—think, —perhaps,—you,—may!"

Chorus of "Oh, good, good; that's perfectly splendid!"

"Aunt Jane, do you know how to make caramels?"

"And cream candy?"

"And cocoanut drops?"

"And butter-scotch?"

"And taffy?"

"And chocolate creams?"

"Well, I must say," said Mrs. King, laughing, "you are very moderate in your demands. Yes, I know how to make all those and ever so many more; but we won't undertake to exhaust my knowledge in this one afternoon. Get your books, and I will write down some of the most favorite recipes."

No. 15—Chocolate Caramels.

Half a pint milk, one and a half ounces (or squares) of Baker's unsweetened chocolate, softened over the fire with as little water as possible; let the milk boil, then stir in the chocolate very hard, add half a pint granulated sugar and two tablespoonfuls molasses; boil until very thick, taking great care not to burn it, pour on well-buttered tins, and when partly cold cut it into small squares.

No. 16—Chicago Caramels.

One cup chocolate, (measure after breaking into small lumps,) one of boiled milk, two of brown sugar, one of molasses, one tablespoonful flour and one of melted butter; boil slowly, until it will stiffen in cold water.

No. 17—Cocoanut Drops.

Grate a cocoanut, take half its weight in sugar, beat the white of one egg to a stiff froth, and stir with it enough of the cocoanut and sugar, well mixed together, to make into small cakes, which should be baked on buttered paper, in a very moderate oven. If any cocoanut is left over, beat another egg and stir in the rest.

No. 18—Cream Candy.

One pound granulated sugar; one-half teaspoonful cream tartar, one wine-glass vinegar; water enough to wet the sugar; flavor to taste with lemon or vanilla. Boil until it will harden in cold water, but not become brittle; it must be tried frequently; then pour into plates, and when nearly cold, pull until it becomes white. If you do not wish to take this trouble, a very good candy can be made by pouring it into a pan and leaving it to harden.

No. 19—Chocolate and Cream Candy.

One .pound sugar, water enough to moisten it; boil until it becomes sugary when stirred in a saucer without water; then take it off the stove and stir until nearly hard. To half the quantity add one ounce grated chocolate, which you must stir in a separate dish; when nearly cold spread the chocolate candy smoothly out in a deep, square pan, well buttered, and the white over it; when cold they will adhere to each other.

No. 20—Soft Candy.

One pound brown sugar, three tablespoonfuls water; while boiling add a quarter of a pound butter; when thick and ropy, take it from the fire and stir till it grains; then pour into buttered plates. For nut candy make the above recipe, stirring in nuts while it is still over the fire.

No. 21—Morrisville Candy.

One pound coffee sugar, one-half pint New Orleans molasses, one-half pint water, two teaspoonfuls butter, one of soda; stir all together and boil till it thickens; when sufficiently boiled it will be waxy.

No. 22—Everton Taffy.

One and a half pounds brown sugar, three ounces butter, one and a half teacups cold water. Boil all together with the grated rind of one lemon, and when cold add the juice.

No. 23—MAPLE CHOCOLATE BALLS.

Crack half a pound maple sugar into small bits, and melt it with a wine-glassful of cold water; when perfectly dissolved let it boil hard for five minutes; while the sugar is boiling, crack the chocolate and put it in a bowl over a boiling tea-kettle; when the sugar is boiled, take it from the fire, put it in a cool place, and beat so stiff that it may be made into balls; flour the hands slightly, and roll into balls of the size of a marble, placing each one, as done, on a buttered plate; when hard, drop them one at a time in the chocolate; turn them carefully with a fork until covered with the chocolate, then place them on buttered paper to cool and harden.

No. 24—MOLASSES CANDY.

One cup molasses, one cup sugar, two tablespoons melted butter, one do. vinegar; boil without stirring until it hardens in cold water, then stir in a teaspoonful soda and pour on buttered tins; when cool, pull and cut into sticks. Never stir molasses candy while it is boiling.

No. 25—BUTTER-SCOTCH.

One cup butter, one of molasses, one of vinegar, a

pinch of soda; boil half an hour, then try by dropping a little into water; if crisp, it is done.

"We made some last winter by a receipt almost exactly like that," said Rose, "and it was perfectly awful. It never got hard at all."

"What kind of molasses did you use?" asked her aunt.

"I don't know; whatever we happened to have."

"You must always take New Orleans molasses for candy. We'll try some with that this afternoon, and I think you won't complain of it. Now here is one that I think is the best of all."

No. 26—CHOCOLATE CREAMS.

One pound white sugar, water to moisten it, half a teaspoonful acetic acid, flavor with vanilla. Try the candy just as for chocolate and cream, (No. 19.) When it is sugary, take it off the stove and stir until nearly hard, then roll into small balls of equal size and put them on a buttered plate to cool. For the coating, put one-half pound chocolate into a pan and set it over a kettle of boiling water; stir until entirely melted. Add a little vanilla, and white sugar enough to thicken, and keep in a warm place. When the white cream-drops

are cold, take a fork and roll them in the melted chocolate; if not smooth let them cool a little, and then form
them with the hand.

"Now," said Aunt Jane, when all this had been written,
"what kind shall we make?"

"Chocolate creams!" said several voices at once.

"Very well; but we have no acetic acid. If you can
pursuade one of the boys to run around to the drug store
and get some, we'll try something else first."

"Butter-scotch is very nice," suggested Mabel.

"And very easy, too," said her aunt; "so you little ones
may cook some of that while we are doing the other. But
do be careful not to burn your dresses! Mamma would
think a plateful of candy a poor recompense for a singed
apron, not to speak of worse mishaps. So I hope you'll
be very careful."

"How delicious it looks," exclaimed Edith, gazing
into the sauce-pan where the cream candy, which they
decided on trying first, was slowly boiling.

"I think it will be good," said Aunt Jane. "But I
must warn you not to be disappointed if you don't suc-
cced well the first time you try it, nor the second. It is

so entirely a matter of judgment to know just how long to boil it, just when it has reached the exact point of 'sugariness' that it really needs long practice before you can do it without a mistake."

"It seems to me you do nothing but try it," said Grace, as she saw her aunt for the dozenth time drop a little of the boiled sugar into a saucer, and, after stirring it awhile, pour it back again. "I shouldn't have the patience to do that so many times."

"Then you will never be a successful candy-maker," said her aunt very decidedly.

By this time the acetic acid had arrived, and the much-desired chocolate creams were begun. "Be sure," said Aunt Jane, while the chocolate was melting, "to stir it only by constantly rubbing it one way, against the side of the pan. Don't stir it round and round. The main body of it should be disturbed just as little as possible."

"Why wouldn't it do to use vanilla chocolate," said Rose, "and not put the vanilla in separately?"

"Because, in the first place, it would be very expensive, and then you don't want sweetened chocolate to make candy of. Melting the sugar in it while it is cooking, is an important part of the process. Now, I think it will be firm enough. Suppose we try a ball, and if it is not, we can boil it a little more."

But it was, and as it was necessary to keep it liquid, the pan was set over hot water at the back of the stove, the result being a most inviting-looking dishful of brown figures of various sorts; for the girls, in defiance of the recipe, had exercised their taste in making cones, lozenges, pipe-stems and various fancy shapes, the rich liquid giving an impartial coating to all.

"There's only one fault to be found with these things," said one of the boys, as he devoured the share which had been assigned to him, "there are not enough of them."

FOURTH DAY.

"Girls, let us give them all a surprise to-morrow," whispered Aunt Jane mysteriously one evening. "Suppose we ask Rhoda to let us cook the breakfast."

"All by ourselves?" asked Mabel with large eyes.

"All by ourselves! That will be the joke of it. How astonished your papa and mamma will be to see a breakfast that their own little daughters have prepared for them! They will think we are getting on famously."

So they all stole out to the kitchen, and finding Rhoda in a good humor, the plan of operations was soon made. The recipes were as follows:

No. 27—VEAL HASH.

Cut off every scrap of fat, gristle and skin from the veal, chop rather fine, and heat together with a small lump of butter, a little milk or cream, and salt and pepper to taste. When done there should be no liquid visible. Serve on toast, which should be dipped in boiling water as fast as toasted, and immediately buttered. Set in the oven or heater until the last moment, as it is very poor when cold. When served for dinner, the dish may be garnished with slices of lemon.

No. 28—Lexington Avenue Potatoes.

Chop cold boiled potatoes as fine as for corned beef hash. Put them in a sauce-pan with a lump of butter and milk or cream enough to cover them; add a little chopped parsley, and salt and pepper to taste. Stir until the milk is quite absorbed, and serve hot.

No. 29—Elmhurst Johnny Cake.

One and a half cups corn meal, half a cup of rice, two eggs, two tablespoonfuls sugar, two heaping do. of butter, three heaping do. of flour, one cup milk, three teaspoonfuls baking powder. Scald the meal until every particle of it has been wet by the boiling milk, then add the rice, and afterward the other ingredients.

No. 30—Plain Omelette.

Take one egg for every two persons at table; beat them well with a pinch of salt and a little parsley; for four eggs a frying pan about the size of a dinner plate will be required. Put a tablespoonful of butter into the pan, and when this is melted pour in the omelette. The moment it begins to cook raise the edge (which will be done first) with a knife, and as soon as the whole is " set " so that no liquid part remains, fold it together and serve. If more than this is required, it will be best to make two omelettes.

"Now I am going to get Rhoda's directions for coffee," said Aunt Jane, "for I don't know any one else who makes it quite so nicely. You must tell us your secret, Rhoda."

"Why, laws, honey," said Rhoda, highly flattered, "I jus' take 'nuf coffee and stir it up with an egg or two, 'cordin' as I happen to have 'em, and put 'bout as much water to it as I think they'll drink, and let it bile till its done. That's all."

"Well, Aunt Jane," said Grace, very gravely, "I suppose I am to write down Rhoda's recipe. Number 31. About enough coffee, some hot water, as many eggs as you happen to have, stir it all up together, and let it boil till its done. Is that it?"

"I think, perhaps, I can make it a little more definite, and easier for other people to understand," said Aunt

Jane, " but I'm afraid I shan't be able to put Rhoda's
judgment into the receipt-book.   The reason why so many
people make poor coffee is that they never find out just
how much coffee to put to just how much water, nor exactly how long to boil it.   Another thing that you are
almost sure to find where the coffee is bad, is that the
coffee-pot is not thoroughly emptied, washed and scalded
after each using.   I have known cooks who never even
threw out the grounds of the day before until they
wanted to use the coffee-pot again for breakfast!   Now
look at the inside of Rhoda's.   You see it has not only
been emptied and washed, but wiped perfectly dry, so
there will be no old, stale taste to mingle with the fresh
one.   I will give you my recipe, which means the same
as Rhoda's."

No. 31—To Make Coffee.

One quart boiling water, half a pint ground coffee, one
egg, half a pint cold water; mix the coffee first with the
egg, (which should not be beaten,) then with the cold
water very thoroughly; put it in the coffee boiler, pour
on the boiling water and let it boil fifteen or twenty minutes, then set it where it will not boil, and throw in one-

4

half gill of cold water. After standing a moment it will be ready to serve. This makes very rich coffee. If it is desired less strong, take less coffee, and cold water in proportion.

"How much is a gill, mamma?" asked Amy.

"A gill is a quarter of a pint; half a tumblerful, or about two small wine-glassfuls," said her mother. "A half gill may be measured by putting four even table-spoonfuls of water into a cup and noticing how high they come up. Then you will always have your measure at hand."

"Is that all we are going to have for breakfast?" inquired Grace.

"You will think it is quite enough when you have done cooking it, Gracie. It is rather an elaborate breakfast. Now if two of you will run and slip on your cooking aprons, we will begin our preparations to-night. We should have to get up almost too early if we should try to do it all in the morning."

Grace and Amy were ready in a twinkling, and while one chopped the cold potatoes left from dinner, the other prepared the veal, and cut it into small lumps ready for mincing. When the potatoes were done, the veal took their place in the chopping-bowl, and after being minced was mixed with a little salt and pepper, and set away in the ice-box for the night.

Bright and early the next morning, the four conspirators, (as Grace called them, because their movements were so secret,) repaired softly to the kitchen, where Rhoda had a good clear fire. Grace set about the Johnny-cake, while Amy ground the coffee, and Mabel beat up the eggs for an omelette.

"You see, Rhoda keeps her roasted coffee in a glass jar," said Aunt Jane. "That is an improvement on the old way of shutting it up in tin canisters, which are much more apt to acquire a stale odor."

"Do the glass jars come on purpose?" asked Amy.

"No, they are meant for preserves, but the reason they are so good for this purpose is that they can be closed up tightly from the air. You see this one can't be opened without the wrench."

When the Johnny-cake went into the oven, Grace took charge of the veal and potatoes at the back of the stove, while the little girls toasted bread at the front. When all else was ready to dish, Mabel turned her omelette into the spider, and it was done in a few minutes and sent in

to the table smoking hot.   Then the girls went to their
rooms to wash their hands and take off their aprons, but
their flushed faces betrayed at the breakfast table that
something unusual had taken place.

"What gave you all such rosy cheeks?" inquired Mr.
Vernon.   "You must have been snowballing, or doing
something of that kind."

"Give you three guesses to find out, Papa," said Grace,
" and if you don't guess rightly you can't have any breakfast."

"Jumping two hundred and fifty times from the roof
of the coal-shed down to the ground," said her father.

"No, not that.   Oh, how far off you are!   You're not
even warm."

"Running races with the steam-cars, to see which
could travel a mile in the shortest time."

"Wrong again!   Why papa, you're perfectly freezing."

"Well, as my breakfast is to depend on it," said her
father, "I think it won't be safe for me to risk another
guess.   I'll turn over my third one to mamma."

It is to be feared that mamma *may* have received a
hint from a glance of Aunt Jane's eyes, for she suggested
quite promptly:

" Cooking the breakfast."

" Right at last! And what do you think of it, now you know who did it?"

" I think it looks superior to any thing they have at Delmonico's, but you don't mean to say you made this coffee?"

" Yes we did—every drop of it! Ask Aunt Jane if we didn't."

" I'll tell you what it is," said Mr. Vernon, " I believe there's some hocus-pocus about this matter. Your Aunt Jane gets behind you some how or other, and takes hold of your hands, just as we do of baby's when we make her write a letter; and you get the idea that you have done the whole thing yourselves."

" No, no, no! It's all honest Indian. She doesn't come near us. She just sits at one end of the table and tells us what to do, and we do it. She never touches a thing."

" I think Aunt Jane deserves a gold medal," said Mr. Vernon.

" I wish we could do something by ourselves this afternoon, without troubling her," said Grace. " Don't you think we are enough advanced now, mamma?"

" I suppose you might make something very simple. How would ginger-snaps do, for instance?"

"Oh, that would be capital!" exclaimed Grace. "We haven't had any ginger-snaps in an age. Are they hard to make, Aunty?"

"Not at all hard to mix up, but they require a good deal of patience to roll and cut out. However, I don't suppose you would mind that."

"Oh, the longer it took the better I should like it! I want to make a good large panful. Please give me the receipt." And Grace drew out her note-book and pencil, which, with a variety of other stores, she always kept at hand in her pocket.

"Do let your aunt finish her breakfast in peace!" said Mr. Vernon. "I won't have her plagued all the time. By and by, Grace, you can attack her again, but now let us think of something else."

Aunt Jane did not wait to be attacked. After breakfast she gave the girls, of her own accord, the recipes which follow.

No. 32—Ginger Snaps.

One cup butter or lard; if only lard is used add a little salt. One and a half cups molasses, one cup sugar, a quarter of a cup sour milk, two teaspoonfuls soda, two do. ginger, flour enough to roll easily.

No. 33—German Puffs.

Take six eggs, leaving out three whites, one pint milk, five tablespoonfuls flour, one of softened butter. Bake in gem pans. Whip the whites of the eggs; afterward stir in the juice of six oranges and half a pound powdered sugar. When the puffs are done, pour the frosting all over them.

No. 34—Dover Cake.

One pound sugar, one do. flour, one-half do. butter, six eggs, half cup milk, half teaspoonful soda.

No. 35—Henry Clay Cake.

One pound flour, one do. sugar, one ounce butter, one-half pint cream, one teaspoon soda, juice and rind of one lemon, one-third of a grated nutmeg. For some tastes the nutmeg is better omitted.

No. 36—Lemon Cake.

One pound flour, one do. sugar, one-half do. butter, one small teacup milk, small teaspoonful soda, four eggs, mix as usual; the last thing before putting in the oven, stir in the juice of a large fresh lemon.

No. 37—Tudor Cake.

Two cups sugar, one-half cup butter, one cup milk three cups flour, three eggs, one teaspoon soda, two cream tartar.

No. 38—Mother's Cookies.

One cup butter, two of sugar, three well-beaten eggs, a quarter of a teaspoonful soda, half a nutmeg, small half-teaspoonful cloves or cinnamon.

No. 39—Ellen's Cookies.

Three-quarters of a cup lard, the same of butter, one cup milk, one teaspoon soda, rind and half the juice of one lemon, just enough flour to roll it out with. Very rich..

No. 40—Plain Cookies.

One pound flour, one-half do. sugar, six oz. butter, three eggs, one teaspoon soda, a little nutmeg or other spice. If richer cookies are desired take one-half pound butter.

No. 41—Bridget's Cookies.

cups sugar, one do. butter, one do. milk, two

eggs, two even teaspoons soda, four of cream tartar; spice if you like it; enough flour to roll easily.

No. 42—Poor Man's Cake.

One cup sugar, two do. flour, one do. milk, one heaping tablespoonful butter, one small teaspoon soda and two of cream tartar, one egg, one-half teaspoonful mixed cinnamon and cloves. . Half a cup of seeded raisins improves it.

No. 43—Ring Jumbles.

One pound butter, one do. sugar, one and a quarter of flour, four eggs. Two tablespoonfuls of any kind of flavoring, or a small wineglass of rosewater. Cream the butter, add the sugar, then the yolks of eggs, then half the flour, then the whites, then the rest of the flour, stirred lightly. Cut out with a tumbler or cake-cutter, and from the middle of each, with a smaller cutter or the top of a canister, cut a round hole. Bake quickly, and sift fine sugar over them as soon as they are done.

No. 44—Plain Jumbles.

One egg, one cup sugar, one-half do. butter, three teaspoonfuls milk, one do. cream tartar, one-half do. soda.

No. 45—Lemon Jumbles.

The above recipe, with the juice and rind of one large lemon, or the juice of two and the grated rind of one.

"There!" said Aunt Jane, when the last one had been written down, "I think I have given you occupation for a long time—that is, if you make up all these good things. Which do you mean to begin on?"

"Oh, please let us make ginger-snaps and some one other kind, and we'll all help each other. Tell us some kind of nice cookies."

"You might better take something that is not to be rolled out, as there is but one rolling-board and pin. Suppose you try Tudor cake? The materials are not expensive, and if you spoil them there will not be much lost."

"Now, Aunt Jane, that's too bad! We're not going to spoil anything! Just examine us and see if we don't know how to put cake together!"

"Well, take that recipe, and tell me how you would go to work."

"First, we'll rub the butter to a cream, then stir in the sugar, then the yolks of eggs; (while one has been mixing

it, the others have been beating the eggs, you know)
then the milk and part of the flour; then—"

"No," said her aunt; "you've left out something."
"Oh, yes; first you measure the cream tartar and sift it
with the flour; then you put the whites of the eggs, then
the soda, *carefully* dissolved in warm water, and poured
off without the dregs; then the rest of the flour, and then
you bake it."

"Very well indeed, and you musn't forget to line your
cake-pan with buttered paper if you want the cake very
delicate, though it is not absolutely necessary. And you
must always warm the pan or cake-tins first. Now tell
me how you'll set about the ginger-snaps."

"Oh, that's easy. Let me see—no eggs; I'll take lard,
because that's easiest; set it near the fire to soften, stir in
the sugar, and then the molasses and ginger; dissolve the
soda in warm water and put it into the sour milk, and
stir *them* in; and then just keep stirring in flour until
you think you can roll it out."

"When it gets too hard to stir with the spoon, you may
mix it with your hand," said Aunt Jane. "But don't
get in too much flour; it wants to have just as little as
possible; and don't forget to flour the pie-board."

"Why do you say 'softened' butter, Mamma, in some of these receipts?" asked Amy.

"Because you never really *melt* butter for cake, even quite common cake; that is, you don't let it turn to oil. The nicest way is to set the cup or bowl with it in, into a pan of boiling water, and then it softens enough to have the sugar stirred into it, which is the main thing. For the more delicate kinds of cake, butter must be rubbed to a cream, either with a wooden spoon or with the hand."

"It seems to me nearly every thing has the juice and rind of a lemon in it," said Mabel.

"Fresh lemons are a great addition to cake," said Aunt Jane, "but you musn't make the mistake of flavoring every thing alike. There are some houses where all their cakes and custards and puddings taste alike, though they have a variety of recipes, because they make every thing with lemon, or nutmeg, or cinnamon, or whatever their taste may incline them to. For instance, I would never put lemon into any two things to be eaten at the same meal. You can have vanilla, or bitter almond, or rose water, or, what is often best, no flavoring at all."

"There is one condition I must positively make," said Mrs. Vernon, as the impatient cooks left the dinner table.

"I can not have Rhoda come back from her 'afternoon out' to find a disorderly kitchen and a great pile of dishes and pans to be washed. If you work in her nice, clean kitchen, you must clear up all traces of yourselves before she comes back."

"Oh, yes, we will," said all at once, and they did it, too, for they knew that if they failed to keep their part of the agreement they would not enjoy the privilege another time. So as soon as Rhoda had washed the dishes and "tidied up," as she called it, in the kitchen, they took possession of her dominions and set to work, after a parting caution from Aunt Jane as to the prime necessity of clean hands and nails.

We need not follow them through the afternoon's operations, which were quite successful, and produced a great dish full of nice ginger-snaps, and two flat, thin pansful of cake. Then they washed the utensils they had used, scraped the flour from the pie-board, and wiped it from the table without spilling any on the floor except a little dusting of it, which was easily disposed of with a broom, and put every article back into its place.

"Why, bless ye, honey," said Rhoda, when Mrs. Vernon asked her about it in the evening, "you wouldn't never have knowed they'd been there at all!"

FIFTH DAY.

"Grace, you and I are invited out to exercise our art to-day," said Mrs. King, one morning. "Your Aunt Carroll has sent over to say that she expects company to lunch; her cook is sick, and the other girl very busy ironing, and as it will be all she can do herself to entertain her friends and see to the table, she would like to have us get the lunch ready, with Rose and Jessie's help, and then I am to be company, and you three girls are to wait on table."

"That will be glorious!" said Grace. "May I write down the recipes now?"

"Yes, and Rose can copy them from your book. We will begin with"

No. 46—CHOCOLATE.

Take two oz. (or two squares) of Baker's chocolate, break it into a little boiling water and stir over the fire until it becomes a smooth paste. If unsweetened chocolate is used, add eight even tablespoonfuls granulated sugar, then add, little by little, a pint of boiling water and a pint of scalded milk. Stir it thoroughly, and allow it to simmer (not boil) for ten minutes; then serve.

No. 47—SARATOGA POTATOES.

Pare raw potatoes; slice them as thin as possible with a potato-cutter (when this is not at hand, they must be *shaved* with a knife); lay them in cold water for an hour or more, then dry them in a towel. Have melted lard at least two inches deep in a kettle; when it is hot cover the surface with the dried slices, sprinkle a little salt over them, turn them with a skimmer, and when done lay them on a doubled brown paper in the open oven. Fry them all in this way, piling them up on the paper as fast as they are taken out of the kettle.

No. 48—CHICKEN CROQUETTES. —

14 oz. boiled chicken, chopped fine, one-half pint milk, a quarter of a ℔. butter, one teaspoonful salt, two even tablespoonfuls flour, a pinch of Cayenne pepper (very small). Mix the flour smooth in a little milk, put the rest of the milk to heat over a saucepan of boiling water, and

when scalded pour in the flour, with the salt, pepper and butter; when like thick cream, mix thoroughly with the chicken and put it aside to become cold and stiff; then make it into twelve long shaped balls, press them perfectly smooth, roll them in beaten yolk of egg, afterward in bread crumbs; fry in lard deep enough for them to swim in.

No. 49—Veal Balls.

One and a half lbs. veal, chopped very fine, three oz. salt pork do., one teaspoonful summer savory, one and a half do. salt, one-half do. sage, two-thirds do pepper; mix thoroughly and make into flat balls. Let them fry slowly in lard or drippings for half an hour.

No. 50—Mixed Croquettes. ―

One chicken, two lbs. veal; boil separately, putting them on in cold water, just enough to cover them. Chop fine with one-third of a loaf bread, season with salt, pepper and a very little mace, beat three eggs light and mix with the above, together with the broth of the chicken; make up in oblong balls and fry in hot lard and butter, equal parts.

"We're not going to make all these to-day, are we, Aunt Jane?" inquired Grace, at this stage of her writing.

"By no means," said her aunt, "but I thought I might as well give you several croquette receipts at once. We can select from among them when we find what materials Aunt Carroll has on hand."

"How can we tell whether a tablespoonful is meant to be heaping or not, mamma, if it isn't water or some such thing?" asked Amy.

"Salt is always to be measured even; also soda, cream tartar and any kind of spice. Of such things as sugar or flour, it is understood that they are to be a little heaped—about as much as the depth of the spoon-bowl, unless it is expressly stated 'even.'"

"What else are we to make for lunch, Aunt Jane?"

"We must have some salad, and for that I will give you recipe"

No. 51—MAYONNAISE DRESSING.

Take the yolk of one egg in a large bowl, and stir it with the right hand, pouring in with the left, not more than a teaspoonful at a time of olive oil, until you have used half a tumblerful; this will make a thick batter.

5

Into the tumbler which contained the oil put half a wine glass of vinegar, a small half teaspoonful of mustard and an even teaspoonful salt; also a dusting of Cayenne pepper, *very* small; mix these thoroughly, and add slowly to the oil batter, stirring all the time. When much salad is used in a family, it is well to make double or treble this quantity, which, if closely covered and kept in a cool place, will keep for weeks.

No. 52—Dresden Dressing.

Rub the yolks of three hard boiled eggs quite smooth; add half a small onion, grated, two tablespoonfuls chopped parsley, one teaspoonful salt, one do. sugar, one small do. dry mustard; mix well, and while stirring fast add a wine-glassful (or a quarter of a tumblerful) of sweet oil; when quite thick, stir in the same quantity of vinegar. This may be used for cold beef, mutton or veal. The meat should be cut into small bits and mixed with the dressing before serving. A palatable lunch-dish.

"I'm sorry you haven't learned to make pastry yet," said Mrs. King, "for some kind of pudding baked in a paste, is an elegant addition to a lunch table. I think your next lesson must be on paste, and then I have some beautiful recipes for you.   There is no time for jelly or blanc-mange; we must substitute some sort of meringue or custard, according to what materials we find ready."

"We shall have to have somebody else's bread, shan't we?"

"Yes, we must have a plate of plain bread, but we ought to have some biscuits or rolls of some kind.   Rolls have to be made with yeast, and that is rather beyond our powers, but we can have popovers or soda-biscuit, or better still, Mrs. Miller's breakfast puffs."

No. 53—BREAKFAST PUFFS.

Three-quarters of a pound flour, one oz. butter, one pint milk, two eggs, one-half teaspoonful salt.   Beat the eggs together and stir them into the milk, pour about two-thirds of the milk on the flour, stirring gradually, that it may be perfectly smooth; melt, and add the butter, and beat very hard for three minutes, then add the remainder of the milk, pour the batter into gem-pans and bake in a very quick oven.

No. 54—GRAHAM POPOVERS.

One pint graham flour, one do. white flour, one

quart milk, two even teaspoonfuls salt, three eggs. Put together exactly like breakfast puffs.

"Then, of course, we must have some cake," said Aunt Jane, "and it musn't be in loaves, for they wouldn't cut nicely so soon after baking. I think Susan's cake is the nicest in the world to eat fresh, but you have made that already, so I will give you some other recipes, and we will select from them afterward."

No. 55—Drop Cake.

Weigh one lb. flour, from which take out three even tablespoonfuls, one lb. sugar, a quarter of a pound butter, one-half pint sweet milk, two-thirds of a teaspoonful soda, two of cream tartar, or one and a half tablespoonfuls baking-powder, five eggs. Butter a dripping-pan, and drop on the batter in separate spoonfuls. Bake in a quick oven.

No. 56—Jelly Cake.

Make drop-cake batter; have ready three well buttered jelly-cake tins, spread them a quarter of an inch deep with the batter and place them in the oven; watch them closely, as they require only a few minutes to bake; have ready three pieces of brown paper on the kitchen table, on which to turn them out, upside down; wipe the pans perfectly smooth, butter and refill them, and while the second set is in the oven spread those on the table with jelly; when the second trio is ready, turn the cakes upside down on the first and proceed as before; the third trio completes the loaves.

No. 57—White Icing.

Beat the whites of two eggs until frothy only, not white; add ten oz. sugar, slowly, with one hand, while you beat with the other. Flavor with lemon juice or vanilla.

No. 58—Chocolate Icing.

Beat the whites of three eggs to a stiff froth, add half a pint of grated sweet chocolate, and half a pint pulverized (not granulated,) sugar.

No. 59—Orange Icing.

Beat the whites of three eggs to a stiff froth; add a quarter of a pound powdered sugar, and the grated rind and soft pulp of two large sour oranges and one lemon. There should be a gill of the juice, (half a tumbler full.) If it makes less than this, add another orange.

No. 60—Orange Cake.

Make and bake drop cake as in the directions for jelly cake, and spread with orange icing; for a top-icing for the whole loaf, more sugar must be added.

No. 61—Chocolate Cake No. 2.

Use the directions for jelly cake, substituting chocolate icing for jelly.

No. 62—Cream Cakes.

Half a pint milk, the yolks of three eggs, one and a half tablespoonfuls sugar, one teaspoonful vanilla, one and a half even tablespoonfuls corn starch. Leave out enough milk to mix the starch with smoothly; boil the rest, and when hot stir in the starch until thicker than boiled custard; then add the other ingredients, beaten together, and continue stirring until it is so thick it will not pour from the spoon, but only drop from it. To do this successfully, the milk must be heated-over, or in, boiling water; never directly on the stove. When the cream is thick enough, proceed as in directions for jelly cake.

No. 63—Number Cake.

One cup butter, two of sugar, three of flour, four eggs, half a cup milk, half a teaspoonful soda and one of cream tartar. A very little spice improves it to some tastes; not more than half a teaspoonful in all of cinnamon, ground cloves and allspice mixed. A variation may be made by putting a whole cup milk, a teaspoonful soda and two of cream tartar. This makes a still lighter mixture.

"Now there is a grand store of recipes to select from," said Mrs. King; "we'll go over and set about our lunch."

Rose and Jessie were watching for them impatiently, and after a little consultation with her sister, Aunt Jane went into the kitchen with her three pupils.

"A hot fire and a tea kettle full of water," said she. "So much is ready at all events."

"I thought Bridget was ironing to-day," observed Grace.

"So she is," said Rose, "but she has her own little charcoal iron-heater in the laundry, and she won't interfere with us at all. And I've found out where everything is, so I can bring out anything you want, Aunt Jane."

"I made out a list of what we should have, Rosie, when I talked it over with your mother. I find she has cold boiled chicken ready, thinking we should want chicken salad; but we are to have croquettes instead; also Saratoga potatoes; lettuce, with Mayonnaise dressing; cold tongue, which was boiled yesterday, and only needs cutting up; tipsy-cake, made with some sponge-cake from the baker's; chocolate, breakfast-puffs and drop-cakes."

" Oh, Aunty! can we *ever* get it all ready in time?"

" I think so; it is only nine o'clock now, and the lunch is not to be served until one. Why, we should be perfect snails if we did not finish it in four hours! Your mamma will set the table before her friends come, so we shall have nothing to do but prepare the eatables. I sent over to her before breakfast, when I first heard that she expected company, to have some potatoes pared and laid in cold water."

" What was that for, Aunt Jane?"

" You'll see presently. Now let us go to work at once. Get the scales, Rose, and weigh out the materials in Gracie's recipe for ' chicken croquettes'; Jessie, you may take the potato-slicer and cut the potatoes, for they have to lie another hour in cold water yet; Grace, I think

you may be trusted to make the soft custard all by yourself; I'll have an eye to you, and tell you if I see anything going wrong."

"Are these the potatoes that puff out like little bal-
loons, Aunt Jane?" said Jessie.

"Yes, the very same; and you shall fry them, too, so
that it will be all your own dish.   Now, Rose, as chopping
the chicken is merely a mechanical operation, and rather
a long one, I'll do that while you get the batter ready to
mix with it."

When this was done, Mrs. King showed Rose how to
make up the croquettes, somewhat in the shape of a
short, fat sausage, and while this was going on, she herself grated the stale bread in which they were to be
rolled.   Then all was set away until it should be time to
cook them.

Next came the Mayonnaise dressing, which was com-
mitted to Grace's care, after she had finished her custard,
and Rose undertook to make some drop-cakes.   Jessie,
who was the youngest, was shown how to make up and
melt the chocolate.   After Grace had finished the salad-
dressing, she set about making the breakfast puffs, according to her recipe, and so the morning wore away
until past twelve o'clock.

"Now it's time to go to work in earnest," said Aunt Jane, whose sharp eyes had been inspecting every operation, while she gave a word of advice to one, of encouragement to another, or of reminder to a third. In the meantime she herself had not been idle, but had cut up a tempting-looking plateful of cold tongue, garnished with pretty sprigs of parsley, prepared the lettuce in a salad-bowl ready to receive the dressing, and neatly trimmed the drop-cakes, which required to be cut apart when they came out of the oven.

"Now for a deep frying-pan of hot lard for the potatoes; Jessie, you mustn't think of another thing but your Saratogas from now to lunch time. Gracie may make the chocolate, now that her puffs are off her mind, and Rose, you must fry the croquettes. As it will be some time before they are ready to turn, you may cut up the sponge-cake and stick it full of those almonds that Jessie is cutting up; then pour the wine over it, and lastly the custard, which must be cold by this time, as it has been standing in the ice-box. Now the grand crisis approaches."

At five minutes before one o'clock everything was finished and ready to "dish"; the girls took off their cook-

ing aprons and washed their hands, then carried in the
hot part of the lunch, all the rest having been previously
placed on the table or the sideboard. "Some time when
we have company at home, and Rhoda gets the lunch,"
said Aunt Jane, "I'll show you girls how to set a table as
beautifully as your mother does, if I can. See how everything has been provided for—not a fork or spoon forgotten! That's one of the great secrets of making any meal
go smoothly."

The bell rang; Mrs. King took her seat among the
guests, and the "three Hebes," as one of the ladies
called them, waited on the table very gracefully and
prettily, according to their previous instructions, which
we will not stop to detail here, as Aunt Jane repeated
them on another occasion. When the grown people had
retired, the waiters took their places at the table, and
though their excitement had prevented them from feeling
hungry while the lunch was in preparation, when they
did finally sit down to it, you would have thought they
had had nothing to eat for a week.

SIXTH DAY.

"You said you would show us how to make pie-crust, Aunt Jane," said Grace one day. "Can't we learn to-day?"

"Just as well as any other day," answered Mrs. King, who was always glad to give pleasure, and was delighted to find that the interest of the little people in cooking was still kept up. "But as that is something that requires not only judgment, but strength, it will not be best for the little ones to attempt it for another year or two yet. You three older ones may begin this morning."

What was the astonishment of the amateurs when Aunt Jane gravely directed them to take all their materials into the cellar!

"To have *perfect* paste," she said, "you must have a cool place to make it in. To-day the kitchen is very hot, and although your pies would taste just as good, the paste would not be so flaky nor look as handsome if it were made so near the fire. In winter it would do very well."

Fortunately, Mrs. Vernon's cellar was dry, airy and well-lighted, so that it was a very pleasant place to be in on a hot day. "There's only one thing more I should like to have," said Mrs. King, " and if I lived next door I would send in and get it; and that is, a marble slab to roll the paste on. I always keep one expressly for the purpose."

" I know the very thing, Mrs. King," said Edith, " and there *is* one next door! When our hall-table slab was broken, Papa had it set out in the shed, and there it is now, just as large as life! May I go in and get it?"

" It would be rather heavy for you, I think; but if you think your mother would not object to our using it, you and Grace may go and bring it, together."

Off flew the girls, and in a few minutes came back in triumph, lugging between them an oblong piece of polished marble, with a great corner broken off, to be sure, but large enough for their purpose. In the mean time, Mrs. King had told Rose to weigh out the materials for the following recipes.

No. 64—Puff Paste.

One lb. flour, three quarters of a lb. butter, one quarter of a lb. lard; salt, ice-water.

No. 65—Plain Pie-Crust.

One lb. flour, a quarter of a lb. butter, a quarter of a lb. lard; or, one cup butter, one cup lard, one quart flour.

"Every thing *must* be cold for paste," said Aunt Jane, again, " so I have had both the lard and butter hardened on the ice, as you see. As we only want two kinds of crust to-day, Rose may make one and Edith the other. Grace can be general helper for the present; by-and-bye we shall find something for her to do."

Each pastry-cook took her station at an end of the table, her materials being neatly ranged near her. A pitcher of ice-water stood between them.

"The beginning is the same for both," said Aunt Jane. "Take the plate with the lard on in your left hand and cut off little bits of lard with a knife, throwing them into the flour as you go along. No matter if they are as small as peas. Now enough salt to make the lard as salt as butter; about half a teaspoonful, I think."

"It seems to me there's salt in everything," remarked Grace.

"Very few things are made without it," answered her

aunt; "nothing, I believe, that contains flour. (Now, girls, stir that lard thoroughly through the flour with a large knife.) We don't put it into preserves or canned fruits, and there are a few things, like blanc-mange, where it is not needed; but it must be added wherever there are eggs or flour, and is always present when any butter is used. Now, you pastry cooks, pour just enough water into the flour and lard to mix it into a loose paste that you can roll out with the rolling-pin. It must all be done with a knife, and as rapidly as possible. Never touch paste with your hands until you begin to roll it."

While this direction was being carried out, Mrs. King gave the girls some of the various notions about making pie-crust.

"Many people—indeed some of the very best cooks—think it quite as well to cut the butter as well as the lard, into the flour, and some people chop them in with a chopping-knife; but I like my old-fashioned way best. Now, Rose, as yours is the puff-paste, you may use the slab first and the others may look on. Sift a dust of flour over your marble pie-board."

"Oughtn't some of the flour to have been kept out for that, Mrs. King?" asked Edith.

"No, that is not necessary when the paste is so rich. A few ounces more than the pound does it no harm. Now turn out the dough from the pan to the pie-board and make it into a compact pile in the middle, all with your knife. That is right; now flour the rolling-pin and roll it down to about half an inch of thickness."

Rose did so.

"I ought to have told you first to divide the butter into four equal parts; that is, as nearly as you can make them so. Now cut the butter into just such little scraps as you did the lard, and spread them evenly over the surface."

"How nice and fresh that butter looks," said Grace.

"It does, indeed," replied Aunt Jane. "And that reminds me of a queer surprise I had when I was in England. I had ordered bread and butter, with some other things, for luncheon, and when the waiter asked me if I would have fresh butter, I said, 'Yes, of course!' taking fresh in an American sense, which means newly made, and, therefore, especially sweet. When they brought it to table I found that it was made without salt!"

"Wasn't it horrid, Aunt Jane?"

"Oh, no, not at all. You were expected to use salt with it, just as you do on your meat and vegetables when they are not salt enough.   Though I think, on the whole, I prefer our fashion.   Now, Rose, you may touch your paste with your hands for the first time.   Sift a dust of flour over the dough that you have spread with butter, then roll it into the shape of a fat bolster.   Now roll it out again thin with the rolling-pin,—not too thin, but rather more than half an inch thick,—then spread on the next portion of butter, sift flour over it, and roll it again, and so on until the butter is all in.   Always roll *from* yourself; don't bring back the pin backwards over the same ground."

"Why not, Aunty?"

"Your paste will not *flake* as finely; and you must remember that I am showing you the most elegant way of making it.   When you don't care to have it look so handsome, or are making it for plain family pies, you can shorten the operation a good deal.   And after making it a very few times, you will not need to weigh or measure at all, except for puff-paste, and many cooks don't do even that.   You learn to *feel* just how much lard and butter are needed in proportion to the flour you have, and much of the trouble is saved."

"What kind of pies are we going to make, Aunt Jane?"

6

"I'll tell you in a minute. Now, Rose, as your last quarter of butter is in, you need not roll it out again just now. Set it in the ice-box till Edith has finished hers. She is to do exactly as you did, except that she need divide her quarter of a pound of butter into only two parts. Don't forget the little sprinkling of flour over it each time you have spread out the butter. Now, as to pies; I thought that, perhaps, to-day I would only let you make puddings."

"Oh, Aunt Jane! then what is all this pie crust for?"— and three pairs of wide-opened eyes were fixed on her at once.

"Perhaps you don't know that a dish only lined with paste and not covered over the top, is a pudding in paste and not a pie at all, always excepting a New England pumpkin pie, of course, or a custard pie; one couldn't call those puddings. But lemon, and cream, and cocoanut, and all such as that, are really puddings."

"How about cranberry, Aunt Jane? That's not covered."

"That is properly a tart; so is a pie made of apples, peaches, or, in fact, any kind of fruit. But as the common custom seems to be against giving any of these things their strictly correct names, I suppose we must go on calling them pies, as the rest of the world do."

"I thought 'tart' meant 'rather sour,' said Rose."

"So it does, in one of its English meanings; but the name as applied to a pie comes from the French. Your paste looks very nice, Edith; now set it in the ice-box while we consider what will be the nicest material to fill our pie-puddings with."

"Then is pumpkin really the only pie, Aunt Jane?"

"Oh, no! all meat pies are properly so named. I don't know when they left off calling them 'pasties' in old England. 'Bring pasties of the doe,' you remember."

"Yes," said Grace, "and when I used to hear Walter spouting Marmion, I thought it was spelt *dough*."

"What a funny idea," said Aunt Jane. "It never occurred to me before. But now I will give you some recipes."

"And are we to call all such pies, 'puddings,' after this, Aunt Jane?"

"Oh, no," said Aunt Jane, laughing; "I only thought I would tell you what you might hear them called at fashionable tables, so that you would not exhibit any surprise. No matter what is set before you, at houses

where you are visiting, and even if it is called by na[m]
that are strange to you, you must act just as if you
been used to it all your life."

No. 66—ESTHER'S LEMON PUDDING.

One cup sugar, one of water, rind and pulp of
lemon, two eggs, half a tablespoonful corn starch.　T[his]
is just enough for one plate.　The eggs must be v[ery]
beaten.　Bake in puff paste.

No. 67—COCOANUT PUDDING.

Half a pound sugar, the same of butter, the same
grated cocoanut, the whites of six eggs, one tablespoon
rose-water, two do. of wine.　Beat the butter and sugar
a cream, beat the eggs to a dry froth and add them, th[en]
the rose-water and wine, and lastly the cocoanut.　B[ake]
in paste.

"That would be a lovely thing to make," said Grace
"It is too rich for family use," replied her aunt, "a[nd]
is rather heavy for this weather; but some time when
are going to have company, and it is a little cooler, y[ou]
shall make it.　Grating the cocoanut used to be a ve[ry]
laborious business, but now that we can get it ready p[re]
pared at the grocer's, it is not so formidable."

"Is it as good, Aunt Jane?"

"Why, no, I can't say that it is, but it saves a vast deal of trouble, and if you are fortunate enough to get it quite fresh, there is not so much difference. Here is another good recipe."

No. 68—Cocoanut Custard Pie.

One lb. cocoanut, half a pound powdered sugar, one quart milk, six eggs well beaten together, half a teaspoonful nutmeg, and two of vanilla or rose-water. Boil the milk, take it from the fire and stir it gradually into the eggs, then add sugar and seasoning, and when nearly cold, the cocoanut. This may be baked in paste or in a dish or cups by itself.

No. 69—Apple Pudding.

Peel, quarter and core enough sour apples to make a pint of apple-sauce when stewed; they must be scantily covered with water; two oz. butter, four do. sugar, a little nutmeg and mace, the grated rind of a lemon, the beaten yolks of two eggs, one wineglassful milk. When all these have been well beaten together, beat the whites of the eggs to a stiff froth, and mix them in lightly. Bake in a paste-lined dish.

No. 70—CUSTARD PIE.

One even tablespoonful corn-starch, two do. milk; put the rest of a quart of milk over boiling water, and when it is scalding (not boiling), stir in the starch carefully, with one-third of a tumblerful sugar and a few grains of salt. When slightly thickened, pour on it four well-beaten eggs (yolks and whites together). Bake in paste. The custard should be an inch deep.

No. 71—ORANGE PUDDING.

One-half pound sugar, a quarter of a pound butter, six eggs, two oranges. Grate the rind from the oranges and squeeze the juice, beat the butter to a cream and add the sugar to it little by little, throw in the yolks of the eggs as you break them, beating them with the mixture, add the orange rind and juice, and finally the whites of eggs, beaten to a stiff froth; these must be added slowly. Bake in paste.

No. 72—MARLBOROUGH PUDDING.

One pint sour apple-sauce, the apples being stewed with only just enough water to keep them from burning, and just long enough to enable you to pass them through a colander; one-half lb. sugar, one-half do. butter, six well-beaten eggs, the juice of two lemons and the grated rind of one. Bake in puff paste.

No. 73—Lemon Pudding.

Half a dozen tart apples, stew and strain through a colander, grated rind and juice of two large lemons or three small ones, one teacup cream, one-half do. butter, two cups sugar, yolks of six eggs. Bake one hour in puff paste.

No. 74—Lemon Pie.

One large or two small lemons, rind and pulp; after the seeds are taken out, squeeze the pulp well in half a tumbler of water, and strain; yolks of four eggs well beaten, one tablespoon flour stirred with the egg, two do. melted butter, the whole well beaten together. Bake until done; then having beaten up the whites of four eggs with three tablespoonfuls powdered sugar, spread it smoothly over the top and set it in the oven a few minutes to brown.

"Now let us look over our recipes," said Mrs. King. "Lemon pudding is always good, and very simple;

apples are not in season, and we have no oranges in the house; the custard pie is nice, but not different enough from lemon to make at the same time. I think we'll have a lemon pie and some puffs of the puff paste, and a raspberry or currant pie of the plainer kind, and perhaps I may think of something else. Grace, see if you think you can make the filling for one of Esther's puddings. They are simple, and always nice."

"I think I can, Aunt Jane," said Grace, looking over the receipt. "I suppose I must wet up the corn-starch with water?"

"Yes, part of the cupful. Be careful not to put in more water than is required, or your pudding won't *stand*—that is, it will be soft and liquid, not firm, like a custard."

"Beat the eggs separately, Aunty?"

"No, that is not necessary, except where it is so stated in the recipe, unless in the case of any kind of nice cake, when the rule is just the reverse. In some lemon pies, only the yolks are put into the mixture, the whites being beaten separately for a cover to the pie; but where this is the intention, you will find it so explained."

So Grace undertook the lemon pudding, and Mrs.

King examined into the condition of the fruit-closet. Here she found a quantity of ripe currants and raspberries, and though she declared it was a pity to spoil anything so nice by cooking it, still, to show the girls what could be done with them, she decided to try two recipes — the following an English one:

No. 75—Currant and Raspberry Tart.

Three half-pints currants, measured after being stripped from the stalks, one half-pint raspberries, three heaping tablespoonfuls crushed sugar; turn a small cup upside down in a deep pie dish, fill the dish with the mixture of currants, raspberries and sugar, cover with puff paste, bake from half to three-quarters of an hour. To be eaten cold, with white sugar sifted over it.

No. 76—Currant Pie.

Line a pie-dish with paste; in it put a layer of currants and a layer of coffee-sugar alternately until full; dredge an even tablespoonful of flour over the top, cover with paste, and bake. All pies of this sort should have a slit cut in the center, and should be well pressed down around the edges.

When the filling for the lemon pie was ready,
King showed the girls how to use the crust. The ar
already made was cut in two and one part rolle
thin; the pie-dish was covered evenly with this.
another plate of the same size was laid, face down
on a thicker layer of paste rolled out on the pie-b
and the shape exactly cut out in paste. This made
cular sheet of paste, from which Grace cut out w
sharp knife a piece from the inside as large as the
portion of the pie-dish, thus leaving a ring of paste
the size of the margin. That already on the plate
then wet, and the other piece laid on it, to make a de
well into which to pour the lemon custard. Then it
ready for the oven.

The English tart came next, and was simply cov
with a layer of pastry, on which, by her aunt's direct.
Grace made some little ornamental quirligigs with s
of paste, and a wavy criss-cross border of the same
ways wetting the part on which an additional layer
paste was to rest, in order to cement them firmly toget
Some puff-paste still remained, which was disposed o
Edith in the following manner:

Being rolled to half an inch in thickness, a numbe

round cakes of the size of the top of a tumbler were cut out. From half of these, smaller circles were cut from the inside with the top of a canister, and the ring thus formed was laid on the other, the under surface being first wetted. These when baked made little hollow puffs, which were filled with jam or jelly and presented quite an elegant appearance.

The remains of the plain pie-crust, after two currant pies had been made from it, was rolled out into short-cakes, with as much flour as they could be made to ab-sorb, and made a welcome addition to the tea-table.

A high authority says that pastry, with the exception of mince-pies, should always be eaten the day it is baked; but as this is not convenient to most house-keep-ers, the expedient of slightly heating the paste just before serving is often practised with good effect.

SEVENTH DAY.

Not long after the last lesson in cookery, Mrs.
was taken ill, and was for some time afterward
ble, requiring to be nourished with special dishe
Grace and Mabel took great satisfaction in prep
her, under their aunt's direction. The first t
they tried their hands at any of this "love-cool
Mabel called it, Aunt Jane gave them a host o
which they afterward made use of as occasion are

"You must always remember," said Mrs. Kin
one of the great points in cooking for the sick, is
things ready exactly at the time they are wante
fifteen or twenty minutes of delay while we are
something in the kitchen, and which passes with
perceiving it, is as long as hours to a sick person.
know at what time anything is ordered, alway
long enough beforehand to allow for not only
but improbable detentions. I shall never fo
mortification I felt when I undertook once to

egg on toast to a sick friend in the evening.   The kitchen
fire was a mass of dead coals and smouldering ashes, and
my only servant was out; even if I could have made up
another fire I couldn't have had any clear coals for toast-
ing, so I made a compromise by holding some water in
a little tin cup over a gas-burner, and half-boiling an egg
.in that!   Then I spread a slice of bread and butter—not
toast!—and emptied the egg over it.   My friend had the
complaisance to eat it; but I know it must have been a
dreadful mess."

"What could you have done any better, Aunt Jane?"
asked Grace.

" I could have told the maid, before she went out, to
leave me a proper fire, which it is never safe to be without when there is sickness in the house; and I could have
had on hand, what I afterwards bought, an arrangement
which fastens on the gas fixture and heats water quite as
soon as the flame of a fire.   To be sure, I could not have
made toast with it, but I could at least have accomplished
a decent poached egg."

" Will you let us make mamma's gruel to-day, Aunt
Jane?"

" Certainly, and as it is not time for it yet, I'll give

you some recipes which you will find useful when you have the care of sick people yourselves, as may happen some time."

No. 77—OLD FASHIONED BEEF TEA.

One pound (or more) of lean beef—(not one scrap of fat must be admitted)—cut into small pieces and put into a tightly-covered jar, without water. Set the jar into a pot of cold water, let this come gradually to a boil and then boil steadily for three or four hours, until the meat is like white rags. Then press the juice out, and season with salt, and, if permitted, a little pepper. This is the pure juice of the meat.

No. 78—LOUISA'S BEEF TEA.

Cut the beef (without fat,) into small pieces, say one inch cube, or thereabouts; put them in an open saucepan over the fire with a very little water—not nearly enough to cover them; take a strong, small iron spoon and press them constantly against the side of the saucepan until you see that every bit of blood is pressed out, and nothing is left but white, leathery lumps; remove these, strain the juice through a hair-sieve, if the broth is required very clear, and flavor as above. An easily made and nutritious food, which can be prepared in fifteen minutes.

No. 79—MRS. MILLER'S BEEF TEA.

One lb. lean, juicy beef, one pint cold water, two even teaspoonfuls salt. Cut the beef in bits about an inch square, cover it with the cold water, and let it stand one hour. Heat it slowly over the fire till it reaches the boiling point, then strain and season.

"They seem to be very much afraid we shall take *fat* beef, Aunt Jane," said Mabel.

"The least particle of fat spoils the tea," answered Aunt Jane, "and as a person is supposed to read over only the one recipe she is using, of course the direction must be repeated each time. But here is something that ought perhaps to have come before the beef tea; in old times it would certainly have done so."

No. 80—INDIAN MEAL GRUEL.

Mix two tablespoonfuls white Indian meal into a thin paste with cold water; stir this into a quart of boiling water, in which has been dissolved one teaspoonful salt; boil it four hours, stir a teaspoonful wheat flour into a cupful of boiling milk (first, of course, mixing it smoothly in a little cold milk), let it boil up once, then add it to the Indian meal and let all boil up once together. If too thick, it is nourishing and tasteful thinned with cream, or if wanted plain, with boiling water.

No. 81—PLAIN GRUEL. ___

Two quarts boiling water; into which stir one cup Indian meal and one tablespoon flour, previously made into a smooth paste with cold water. Boil slowly one hour. A handful of raisins boiled in the gruel improves it, especially for children's taste.

No. 82—OATMEAL GRUEL. —

Mix two tablespoonfuls oatmeal with three of cold water; pour on one pint boiling water, then boil five minutes, stirring all the time; skim, and strain through a hair-sieve. Farina gruel is made in the same way.

No. 83—RICE GRUEL.

Mix two tablespoonfuls ground rice smooth with cold water, stir it into a pint of boiling milk; boil until it is as thick as good cream; sweeten to taste, and grate in a little nutmeg.

" In every recipe where meal of any kind is stirred into boiling milk," said Mrs. King, " it is better to pour the milk into the dish containing the meal, then turn the whole back into the saucepan. It is very difficult to keep porridge from getting lumpy if you stir in the flour while the milk is over the fire."

No. 84—Imitation of Asses' Milk.

Put into a saucepan one half-pint milk and the same of water; while they are coming to a boil, beat up two eggs very light, yolks and whites together; pour the boiling mixture on the egg, but do not boil afterwards; sweeten with white sugar-candy.

No. 85—Panada.

To one gill (or half a tumblerful) of wine, add one and a half tumblerfuls boiling water; flavor with nutmeg or lemon and sweeten slightly. Stir in grated bread or crackers to make it as thick as gruel, and let it boil up once.

No. 86—Rice Blanc Mange.

Four tablespoonfuls ground rice and one saltspoon salt, wet with cold milk and stirred into one quart boiling

7

milk. Rub the rind of a lemon hard with lump sugar,
and sweeten with the sugar thus flavored. Boil, stirring
all the time, for eight minutes; then cool it, and add the
whites of three eggs beaten to a froth. Place over the
fire again and stir constantly until boiling hot, then turn
into moulds to harden.

No. 87.—TAPIOCA JELLY.

Soak two oz. tapioca five hours, or over night, in half a
pint of cold water; put it over the fire with another half
pint cold water, and when quite thick add half a tumbler
boiling water; let it boil until the pieces look perfectly
clear, then add four tablespoonfuls sugar, and flavor with
two teaspoons brandy or two tablespoons wine. If lemon
is preferred, boil the rind of one with the tapioca until it
is flavored, and add some of the juice, if the flavor is
liked so strong. Pour it into small moulds wet with
water, and set it on the ice.

" Why must the moulds be wet, Aunty? "

"To prevent the tapioca from sticking to them. In
turning out moulds of jelly or blanc-mange, you know, we
warm them outside with a towel wrung out of boiling
water, or set them for a moment into a pan of hot water,

to melt the surface next the mould; but tapioca is so
sticky, this is not always sufficient."

No. 88.—ARROWROOT GRUEL.

One oz. arrowroot, mixed smooth in cold milk and
stirred into one pint boiling milk, with one heaping teaspoon sugar, and a pinch salt; stir until it is thick as
cream, then cool a little, and serve.

No. 89.—ARROWROOT JELLY.

Wet two heaping teaspoonfuls Bermuda arrowroot in a
little cold water, then stir into one cup boiling water, in
which two teaspoonfuls white sugar have been dissolved.
Stir until clear, boiling steadily, then add the lemon. Wet
a cup with cold water and pour in the jelly to stiffen.
To be eaten cold with sugar and cream. The same recipe, made with milk instead of water and one additional
teaspoonful of arrowroot, makes a delicious blanc-mange.
It must be boiled until well thickened.

"Don't they always give sick people chicken-broth,
Aunt Jane?" asked Mabel.

"When the sick people begin to get well, they generally do, my dear," replied Mrs. King. "I am just coming to that receipt."

No. 90.—CHICKEN BROTH. ⁓

Boil an ordinary sized chicken in two quarts unsalted water, cracking the bones well before putting in the fowl. Cover it closely, and boil until the meat all falls to pieces. The water must be cold when the chicken is put in. When done, strain the broth, to which add one tablespoonful rice or pearl barley, soaked in a little warm water, and simmer half an hour; then add four tablespoons milk, some salt and pepper and a little chopped parsley, and simmer five minutes. Be careful not to oversalt, but carry up a small salt-cellar on the waiter with the broth. Serve with dry toast.

No. 91.—BEEF AND SAGO BROTH.

Two lbs. beef cut up small into two quarts cold, unsalted water; stew until the beef falls to pieces; strain it out, add salt and one cup sago, carefully washed and soaked until soft in a little lukewarm water. After the sago is in, simmer one hour, stirring often. Then add the beaten yolks of three eggs; boil up once and serve with dry toast.

No. 92—BEEF STEAK

Broil one lb. of tender, juicy beef
son with salt and pepper; cut it i
on a pint of boiling water, steep
press well, and pour off the liquid

No. 93—BEEF SAND

Scrape or chop fine a little raw
juicy piece; season with pepper and
thin slice of thinly buttered bread;
slice, and cut into three or four neat
cording to the size of the loaf.

"Raw beef!" exclaimed Grace, "that
I hope nobody will ever give me any!"

"Most people find it exceedingly nice, (
you had such a sandwich put into your h
knowing what it was made of, I've no doub
do the same. Raw beef is very nourishing
digested; that is why it is recommended for sic

No 94—TOAST-WATER.

Toast two thin slices of bread thoroughly, but wi
burning them. It is a great mistake to think that t

ly do, my dear," re scraped off, is as nice as that
to that receipt."   at first.   While hot, pour one
                        es, and let them stand in a c
                No. 9

Boil an ordinary siz
water, cracking the bo 95—Egg Nog.

Cover it closely, and b egg in a tumbler, with tw
The water must be the same of sugar, measured
When done, strain th y froth, mix it thoroughly wit
ful rice or pearl barl s with milk.
simmer half an hc may be made on this recipe.
some salt and pep egg, but must have brandy and
simmer five min ot use milk, but take the brandy
carry up a small hile others again, and they, perhap
Serve with dry best nourished by an egg beaten up
                a half the stated quantity of sugar, s
                rich milk or cream.
Two lbs.

salted wat No. 96—Flax-seed Lemonade.

out, add ir even tablespoonfuls whole flax-seed,
soaked ar one quart boiling water.   Let it stand
sago in a covered pitcher, then add the juice o
beat s, and sweeten to taste.   If too thick, thin w
dr cold water or ice.

"Aren't there any recipes for making cocoa, Aunt Jane?" asked Grace.

"Yes, plenty; but as they are sure to come on the packages of cocoa, or broma, or 'racahout des Arabes,' or alkethrepta, or whatever other name the preparation is called by, I don't think it worth while to give you any. There is one drink, though, I used to think delicious when I drank it fresh from the mill where it was made—cocoa shells. Did you ever see any?'"

"No; I never heard of them."

"I've no doubt that they are to be had at the grocers, and I'll give you the directions. Miss Bremer, when she was in this country, used to call this drink, ' De nectar of de gods.'"

No. 97—Cocoa Shells.

One quart boiling water, two oz. cocoa shells, sometimes called *nibs*, wet first with a little cold water; boil an hour and a half, strain, add one quart milk (better if you can have it part cream), let it heat nearly to boiling, then take off and serve.

"Now, as the doctor said Mamma might eat a little something besides her gruel to-day, suppose we try how

she likes a poached egg on toast, with a cup of
will be a pleasant little surprise to her."

The girls were delighted with the thought, and
the kitchen half an hour before the time of servir
to be sure not to be late. There was a bright, clear
largest egg was picked out and the loaf brought
the bread-box, ready to cut.

"Here's some lovely fresh bread," remarked
when her aunt came in.

"Oh, fresh bread wouldn't toast well at all! I
be all rough and crumbly. Ask Rhoda if she
some about two days old. If she hasn't any mo
than this, we must send round to the baker's."

Fortunately another visit to the bread-box d
some just in the right condition.

"Now get the waiter ready; a clean napkin for
a great dinner napkin that will hang down eve
over the sides—a fringed one will be prettier;
little tete-a-tete set that mamma had for a Christm
ent. Ah! they are rather dusty, they haven't be
for so long; you must wash and wipe them. Wh
clean napkin? Don't put it in the ring; lay it
side of the plate and get the smallest salt-cellar.

fill the little sugar-bowl about half full of sugar and the cream-jug the same; a small knife and fork,—yes, I think that's all. Have a plate of butter on the table ready for the toast, and a large bowl for boiling water to dip it in; we'll make the tea first. The old rule is, a spoonful apiece and one for the pot, but that allows for two cups, and mamma will want only one, so one teaspoonful, a little heaped, will be plenty."

"Shall we make it in the little tea-pot, Aunt Jane?"

"No, we must take Rhoda's steeper, for this is English breakfast-tea, and must be boiled a few minutes. Oolong, or any kind of green tea, should only be steeped, but you cannot get the full flavor of this kind without boiling it. Scald the steamer first and throw out the water; now put in the tea and pour on about half a pint of boiling water from the tea kettle, then set it where it will simmer for five minutes. Now you may toast the bread, Mabel; you see Rhoda has cut a beautiful even slice. Grace, pour some boiling water into this frying pan, then break the egg very carefully into a saucer, and slide it off into the hot water."

Grace did so, and then her Aunt told her that she must not try to poach eggs in water that was boiling

hard, or they would fly in pieces. The water mns
boiling to begin with, but afterwards merely simmer
til the white was cooked so that no liquid part remai
then the yolk would be sufficiently done. By the
this was done, Mabel's toast had been dipped and
tered and laid on the plate; the egg was then caref
lifted off with a skimmer and placed upon it, cov
with a large bowl, the tea poured off the leaves into
little tea-pot, a small pitcher of hot water added in
it should be too strong, and then Grace, being the ta
started off with the waiter, Mabel going along for c
pany.

"Whatever else you do, girls," said Aunt Jane, as
were on the way, "*don't* make tea with water that doe
boil! There is more wretched stuff drunk under
name of tea, from this cause, than from any other. M
a girl I have had say to me, 'Why, it *has* boiled!' w
I saw from the looks of the tea that it hadn't been m
with boiling water. The idea that it must actually
boiling hard at the moment it touches the leaves, is
most impossible to get into their heads."

At the door of the sick room Mabel took off the b
that had covered the toast and egg, and put it on a t

in the hall, and the little girls were rewarded by a smile from their mother, and by hearing her remark that nothing had tasted *quite* so good to her since she had been sick as this little meal of her daughters' preparation.

EIGHTH DAY.

"Oh, mamma, what *do* you think?" said Grace,
ing into the breakfast-room one morning. "M
has invited——"

"Good morning, my dear," said Mrs. Vernon, ch
the torrent of words with a motherly smile. ".
is the first time we have seen you, we should lik
little piece of courtesy as an introduction to wh
have to say."

"Good morning, mamma; good morning, Aunt
Mr. Lane has invited all our three families, bo
babies and grown people and everything, to go to
nic in his woods out in the country on the Fourt
it isn't to be a general basket pic-nic, but Mrs. I
going to send all the lunch from her house, and she
to know if Aunt Jane and all of us girls won't go
Monday afternoon and make the things, and if we'
her a list of what's wanted, she'll have everything r

"I don't wonder that you are out of breath, Grac

that long speech; do sit down and rest a few minutes. If your papa says yes, we'll go to the pic-nic with pleasure, and as for having a cooking-party at Mrs. Lane's, you must ask Aunt Jane about that."

"Oh, I know Aunt Jane will say 'yes,' she's such a dear, good, kind, *first-rate* Aunty! Won't you, Aunt Jane?"

"After all that praise, I'm afraid I might lose my reputation for amiability if I said 'no,'" said Mrs. King, laughing; "but luckily, I don't want to say no. I think the notion is capital, and I am for accepting at once."

"Oh, you best of aunts!" exclaimed Grace, embracing her aunt rapturously. "I'll run and tell Mrs. Lane now —may I, mamma?".

"I think Mrs. Lane will be able to wait until after breakfast," answered Mrs. Vernon, "and you must remember that you haven't consulted your father yet."

"Oh, I know beforehand what *he'll* say; 'Just as your mother pleases.' I haven't asked papa's consent to any thing a thousand times in my life not to know that by this time. I hope he'll come down soon, though, so I can go through the motions."

As Grace had foretold, her father made no objections,

and in the course of the morning Aunt Jane went into Mrs. Lane's to arrange with her about particulars.

"Well, Aunt Jane, what are we to have?" inquired Grace when her aunt came back.

"Oh, we have arranged a very nice bill of fare; but never mind going over it now. I will just give you some new recipes, and we can talk over the rest of the programme afterwards."

No. 98—VEAL LOAF.

Three lbs. raw veal and half a lb. raw pork chopped fine together; three Boston crackers rolled fine, or a cup and a half of bread crumbs; three eggs, one teaspoonful black pepper, a very little sage, the same of mace, one teaspoonful salt. Pack into square tin pans; strew bread crumbs or grated cracker over the top, and while baking, baste with a tablespoonful of butter dissolved in boiling water. Bake three hours in a moderate oven.

"What is 'basting,' Aunt Jane?" asked Grace.

"Pouring liquid over something that is baking or roasting. This keeps it moist, and cements the other ingredients together."

"What is the difference between baking and roasting?"

"In old times it used to be called baking when things were cooked in an oven, and roasting when they were placed before the open fire on a spit, or what is called a 'Dutch oven'—a tin arrangement with only the side toward the fire open, so that the whole heat, direct and reflected, might be concentrated on the meat; but in these days when there are very few open fires, every thing is baked, and it is generally said that meat is roasted, and all other things baked, in the oven.   Here are some cake recipes."

No. 99—French Cake.

One pound sugar, one-half do. butter, one do. currants, dredged with flour, three cups flour, four eggs; spice to taste, half a teaspoonful soda dissolved in three tablespoonfuls milk.

No. 100—Loaf Cake.

Two cups risen dough taken from bread after its second rising.   Have ready two cups sugar, one do. butter, three eggs, one teaspoonful soda, two tablespoonfuls milk or cream, half a pound seeded raisins, one teaspoonful cloves, half as much grated nutmeg.

No. 101—FRUIT GINGERBREAD.

Two lbs. flour, three-quarters do. butter, one
coffee-sugar, one do. raisins, one do. currants, two cu
molasses, one-half do. sour cream (or milk, if you cani
get cream), six eggs beaten separately, one heaping t
poonful soda, two tablespoonfuls ginger, one teaspoon
cinnamon and one of cloves. Cream the butter and sug
warm the molasses a little and add to them; next t
beaten yolks, then the the milk and spice, soda, flour a
whites, well beaten; last, the fruit, which must be dredg
with flour. Beat all together well, the last thing bef
baking. Bake in two loaves, in a moderate oven. T
cake will keep a long time.

No. 102—PLAIN GINGERBREAD.

One cup butter, one do. sugar, one do. molasses, o
do. sour milk, two eggs, one teaspoonful soda, one of ci
namon, and one tablespoonful ginger, nearly five cups
flour. Be careful not to get it too hard; it should be abo
as thick as cup-cake batter.

No. 103—SPONGE GINGERBREAD, WITHOUT EGGS.

Three cups flour, one of molasses, one of sugar, one

milk (sour is best), one heaping tablespoonful butter, two teaspoons saleratus (not soda), two do. ginger, one do. cinnamon.   Mix the molasses, sugar, butter and spice together; warm them a little and beat until they are very light in color; then add the milk, the saleratus, and lastly, the flour.   Beat hard five minutes and bake in shallow pans, or, if preferred, in small cake-tins.

No. 104—TEA-BISCUIT.

One quart flour, two heaping tablespoonfuls lard, two cups milk (new milk, if you can get it), one teaspoonful soda and two of cream tartar, one saltspoon salt.   Sift the cream tartar into the flour, then put in the salt, then the lard, rubbed lightly through the flour with the hands, next the soda, dissolved in a little of the milk, then, as rapidly as possible, the rest of the milk.   Knead all together as fast as you can, roll out lightly and cut into cakes at least half an inch thick.   Bake in a quick oven.

"Now, I believe I have given you all the receipts we shall need," said Mrs. King, "besides a good many others. You know we have a pretty large party to provide for; eight from here, three from Mrs. Lane's, and five from

Aunt Carroll's—sixteen hungry people! Here is our bill of fare, that she and I made out together.

"Veal loaf, ham-sandwiches, potato salad, buttered biscuit, short-cakes, black cap and huckleberry pies, loaf cake, soft gingerbread, iced tea and coffee for the grown folks."

"And what shall *we* have to drink, Aunt Jane?"

"Oh, I think little folks can get on very well with ice-water. However, there is a very nice preparation called lemon sugar, that makes a pleasant drink when mixed with water, and we'll take along a bottle of that. I advised Mrs. Lane against lemonade, it is so troublesome and hard to manage."

"Are we going to make every thing to-morrow?"

"Mrs. Lane will have the veal and pork weighed and chopped up at the butcher's, and the ham boiled to-day for the sandwiches, and as her cook is going to bake bread to-morrow, we shall have some light dough ready for the loaf-cake; every thing else I think we can prepare ourselves."

The next morning saw a busy scene at Mrs. Lane's. Six clean-aproned little girls bustled about the kitchen, like peas on a hot shovel, somebody said; Ellen, the cook, had to be on hand to give out materials and utensils. Mrs. Lane said she could *not* keep out of the kitchen, it was so delightful to watch them, and Aunt Jane sat by a corner of the table up against the wall, in the character of the Genius of the place, inspiring every one with the power suited to the occasion.

"The dough will be ready for your loaf-cake very soon, Edith; you must be ready for it. Take your recipe and put the materials together just as we always do, and Mabel and Amy will stone the raisins."

"Shall we weigh them first, Aunt Jane?"

"No, raisins musn't be weighed until after the seeds are taken out. Rose, you may set about the veal loaf; the meat is all ready, mixed by the butcher; Ellen will give you some bread to crumb up, and you can see by your recipe what else you will want."

"I'm waiting patiently for my turn, Aunt Jane," said Grace.

"Yes, I see. You may have either the soft ginger-bread or the pies for your share. Which will you take?"

"Oh, the pies, if I may make them all alone! May I go into the cellar and do it all by myself?"

"Yes, if you want to," said Mrs. King. "But wouldn't you rather have a little oversight and advice?"

"No, I just want to take all the responsibility myself. I don't want anybody to see them until they go into the oven."

"Very well, just as you like. The berries are all nicely looked over and clean; all you have to do is to be careful not to put in too much sugar, as they are both so sweet."

"I wish pie-crust could be measured instead of weighed," sighed Grace. "It's *so* much trouble."

"Oh, I can give you a nice receipt for measuring if you are not afraid to try it for the first time by yourself. Here it is:"

No. 105—Cup Pie-Crust.

One cup butter, one of lard, four cups flour.

"Is that all?" said Grace. "What a comical little recipe!"

"Of course it is understood that you know how to put it together, and also that you will add about half a tea-spoonful of salt on account of the lard, and make it up with ice-water. Don't forget, too, after the under crust is on and the fruit in, to wet the margin of paste that will be touched by the upper crust, so as to make it keep together, and as we don't want very rich paste, make your

cups of flour rather large, and those of butter and lard
rather small."

Grace went off in high glee, and Mrs. King turned to
Jessie.

"Here is a good little girl who can chop the ham for the
sandwiches if Ellen will cut some slices for her. Of
course we can't make them before to-morrow morning,
but the ham can be chopped and shut up tight in a cold
place, and it will be quite as good. The bread that is just
going in to bake will be exactly right to cut up by that
time."

"I never heard before of chopping ham that was to go
in sandwiches," observed Ellen; "I always saw the slices
just put in whole."

"And did you ever see any one try to bite through a
good thick piece of ham and two slices of bread, Ellen?"
said Mrs. King. "I have, and dreadful work they made
of it. Some people are so particular that they grate the
ham, but I think it is just as good chopped up into rather
small pieces; not too fine, Jessie, but about a quarter of
a mouthful."

When Mabel and Amy had finished stoning the raisins,
Mrs. King set one of them to making the salad dressing,

and the other to measuring the ingredients for the ginger-bread, using the dishes which Edith had for the cake, so as to save the trouble of washing.

"And when the cake is finished and set to rise in the baking-tins," said Aunt Jane, "You can mix your ginger-bread up in that same pan she has it in now."

This was the recipe for the salad dressing:

No. 106—SIMPLE SALAD DRESSING.

One teaspoonful salt, small half teaspoon pepper, the same of dry mustard, two tablespoonfuls finely chopped parsley, a taste of grated onion, one gill of vinegar and the same of oil. Cut up cold potatoes, boiled not too long, but firm and solid, into small mouthfuls, pour the dressing over them and let them stand in it half an hour before serving.

"Ellen must save out some of the potatoes she cooks for dinner," said Mrs. King, "and not boil them quite as long as the others."

"But we have new potatoes, ma'am," said Ellen.

"Oh, those will be delicious! Save the very smallest for us—all the little buttons you can pick out. Those that are too large for mouthfuls can be cut into two or three pieces."

When Rose had finished the veal loaf and packed it in
the pan, ready to go into the oven when Ellen's bread
should come out, she set about trying a new recipe.

No. 107—Grandma's Short-Cake.

One pound sifted flour, dried in the oven for a few minutes, but not browned, a quarter of a pound butter, a
heaping tablespoonful lard, a salt-spoonful salt, a pinch
of soda dissolved in just enough vinegar to cover it
and well worked in. Put together with ice-water, and
roll out half an inch thick. Cut into squares, prick with
a fork and bake light brown.

"How *can* any one tell how much a pinch is, Aunt
Jane?" asked Rose. "Is it about as much as when you
take a pinch of anybody's arm?"

"Oh, no," said her aunt, laughing, "a pinch is just
about so much," showing her by taking up some soda between her finger and thumb. "A pinch is a pinch, that's
all. A cook gets to feel those things after a while.
There's a sort of instinct about it."

"Now the salad dressing is done, aunty," said Mabel.
"What shall I do with it?"

"Ask Ellen for a funnel, and we'll pour it into this bottle and cork it tightly. We musn't forget to take along a small bottle of vinegar, too, for some people, especially children, don't like so large a proportion of oil."

"May I make the biscuit now?" asked Edith, when her loaf-cake was kneaded into loaves and set to rise in the pan.

"Better wait until the bread comes out. The gingerbread is in already, and we must leave a place for Grace's pies. Your biscuits will contain soda, you know, and so musn't stand a moment after they are mixed before they go into the oven. I wonder what keeps Grace so long at her pies; it seems as if they ought to be ready by this time."

It was not long before Grace came in, a pie carefully balanced on the palm of each hand. A glance at their extremely ornate appearance explained the delay. In the middle of one she had made not a bad imitation of a rose, whose paste leaves stood out quite naturally; around this was a series of rings laid over one another like shingles, producing a very pretty effect, and round the edge was a border made of long strips interlaced so as to make a sort of braid. The other was bordered with a series of little buttons, touching one another; inside of this was a circle of leaves quite neatly made, with a slender vine connecting the ends, and in the center in fat letters and figures was the date, "July 4, 1876."

"Why, Grace, what a pie-ist you are!" exclaimed her brother Rob, who had stolen in to take a peep at the doings of the busy bees. "You're the Great Champion American Ornamental Pie Constructor, and no mistake. That pie's too fine to eat; let's send it to the Centennial."

"You may send your piece there if you like, Rob," said his aunt, "but the rest of us would prefer to eat ours ourselves. Now, Edith, Ellen says it is safe for you to make your biscuit, and when that comes out, our work will be done for to-day."

A new idea came into Aunt Jane's head, however, and she whispered privately to Edith, "I'm coming over by-and-by to contrive a little surprise for the rest of them. Do you have sixteen nice large eggs ready after dinner and some boiling water."

So in the afternoon she slipped over alone, and telling Mrs. Lane she wanted to have a private conference with Edith, proceeded to the kitchen. First she gave her this recipe:

No. 108—Stuffed Eggs.

Boil eggs hard; take off the shells without breaking the whites, cut the eggs neatly in two in the middle, take out the yolk and rub to a powder, which mix with salt, pepper and dry mustard. Fill each hollow with this mixture, then place the ends together again and wrap in tissue paper. A picnic dish.

"Now put on the eggs where they will boil gently for ten or fifteen minutes. You know if the water boils violently they will knock against one another and crack the shells, and that would spoil the shape of them. While they are boiling we will cut this paper, if you will get some scissors."

Aunt Jane had brought with her several sheets of white tissue paper, and she showed Edith how to cut the ends in fringe like motto-papers. "We'll not wrap the eggs in them to-day," said she, "but have them ready for the morning."

When the eggs were boiled, the shells were carefully picked off according to directions, and the beautiful, smooth white balls cut in two. Mrs. King said there were no particular directions about mixing the condiments.

A teaspoonful each of black pepper and dry mustard, with two of salt, would, she thought, be enough. When the whites were refilled and carefully placed on their ends in a dish, touching each other closely that they might not lose shape, it was found that there was still a considerable quantity of the seasoned yolk left.

"We'll put that into the salad-dressing," said Aunt Jane. "It can't hurt it, and it may make it a little nicer. I shall be in here again the first thing to-morrow morning."

There was not much left to be done the next morning. Aunt Jane went in very early to Mrs. Lane's to superintend the making of the sandwiches.

"They *must* be cut thin, and they *must* be small," said she to Edith, "if you want them to be good. Those dreadful lumps of thick bread with great mats of ham between that some people mistake for sandwiches, are fit only for savages, and ours are to be eaten by civilized beings."

Then she showed Edith how to butter the bread, so that the slices should exactly fit, one on the other; the chopped ham was scattered thickly over the lower one, a little mustard wet up with vinegar was sprinkled lightly

upon it, and then the matching slices were neatl
down and pressed together. Afterward each doul
was cut into several pieces, easy to be handled.

Then the biscuits were split and buttered, a
stuffed egg was wrapped in its piece of tissue
The tea and coffee were first turned into pitchers
cream was added with a moderate amount of sug
then poured into bottles, which were made secure by
a piece of cloth tied down tightly over each cork.
additional sugar was carried along in a well-washe
bottle, this being more easily managed than a pap
a supply of salt was not forgotten.

"I can't imagine," said Mr. Lane to Mrs. King,
were all seated at their pleasant lunch in a shady
"how you have managed to remember everything
idea of a picnic is that some of the most import
ticles are always found to have been left behind wl
time comes to use them."

"I always begin by making a list of everythin
can possibly be needed," replied she. "At
where we have these gipsy parties very often, I
permanent one, and just vary it as occasion requi
never feel safe without it, because it is often the m

vious things that are forgotten, every one thinking them a matter of course. Now, we have reduced gipsying to such a system that our picnics are nearly as well served as our dinner-tables."

It is pleasant to be able to say that the good things which our young friends had expended so much labor upon proved very satisfactory. The veal loaf was especially liked, while Grace's ornamented pies and Edith's pretty stuffed eggs were much admired by the young people. There was only one thing that would have pleased them better; they would have liked to do some of the cooking on the spot.

"That's all very well for young ladies and gentlemen who want to make a frolic of it," said Aunt Jane, "but we old folks like to rest when we get out into the woods; we don't want to work. If I have to do that, I'd rather it should be in my own comfortable kitchen."

"I can tell you we're very thankful to have such a pleasant excursion as this, any way you like to manage it, Aunt Jane," said Rose, speaking for the rest; and they all agreed with her.

NINTH DAY.

"Dear me!" said Mrs. Vernon, in a despairing
she saw from her bedroom window a carriage dri
the door; "there's Mrs. Harvey and her two d
come in from the country to lunch, and there
thing in the house! I told Rhoda she might s
day out, and we are to have a six o'clock dinner
Mr. Vernon wasn't to come to lunch, I thought w
just have a cup of tea and some bread and butter
serves for lunch. What shall I do? They'll be
after their journey."

"Just leave it to me," said Mrs. King, whom
dressed. "Lend me the girls to help cook, and l
set the table, and you shall have lunch in half an

"I know you can do wonders, Jane, but I don't
you can get up anything with what you'll find
house!" said Mrs. Vernon.

But Mrs. King was already far on her way to th
en, where her sister sent the three girls to join he

cake in the house," said Mrs. Vernon, after her friends were gone; " but to-day happened to be one of the times."

" Why can't we make some this afternoon, mamma?" inquired Grace, whose taste for cooking seemed to grow with exercise, instead of wearing off as her mother had feared it would,—" though I don't believe any one missed the cake at all, for they all seemed to enjoy their lunch very much."

" I think your idea is a good one, Gracie," said Mrs. King, " and I have some nice recipes that we haven't tried yet; so if mamma has no objection, we'll do as much as we have time for. What are you going to have for dessert? "

" I haven't the slightest idea," said Mrs. Vernon, " I suppose Rhoda will make a pudding of some sort."

" Well, if we happen to think of anything nice, we'll make it, and Rhoda won't object to having some of her work done beforehand. Come, girls, on with your aprons again, that is, if you want to, and we'll see what we can do."

The little girls had become such enthusiasts in the matter of cooking, that this invitation was never given in vain, for Aunt Jane was a charming companion, and en-

9

livened the hours passed in the kitchen with such pleasant conversation that they wanted no better amusement.

"I wish we could make some blanc-mange," said Mabel. "I like that better than anything else."

"It is too late to have that to-day," replied Aunt Jane, "because it wouldn't have time to get hard. We can make some for to-morrow's dessert, but even then we must use farina or corn-starch, because gelatine needs to soak for a long time. Most people prefer these because there is more body to them; but I will give you some recipes for both kinds."

No. 109—BLANC-MANGE. ———

One quart milk, one oz. Cooper's gelatine or isinglass, two teaspoonfuls vanilla, three-quarters of a cup sugar. Keep out one cupful of the milk, and soak the gelatine in it for not less than an hour; scald the rest of the milk, and pour into it, afterward heating (not boiling), all together until the gelatine is perfectly dissolved. Stir frequently, then add the sugar and pour into moulds wet with cold water. To be eaten with cream, boiled custard, or any kind of preserves or canned fruit.

"It doesn't tell what kind of sugar you must take," remarked Mabel.

"I use granulated sugar for almost all kinds of cooking," replied Aunt Jane. "It is so easy to manage. For hard pudding-sauce, or for sifting over the top of pies or cake, you should have powdered; and for ginger-bread or any kind of cake or pudding made with molasses, coffee sugar is nicest, unless brown is expressly mentioned. Here are some more receipts for you."

No. 110—Farina Blanc-Mange.

One quart new milk, two ounces farina, half a salt-spoon salt. Put the milk over boiling water, keeping out a little to mix with the farina. When the hot milk has a film over it, add the farina and salt, and stir until it forms quite a thick batter; then pour into moulds wet with cold water.

No. 111—Chocolate Meringue.

Dissolve three tablespoonfuls corn-starch in two table-spoonfuls milk; break up two ounces of sweetened chocolate in a tin basin over boiling water, and to it add gradually the rest of a pint of milk; stir until perfectly smooth, and when it is scalding, pour in the starch and stir till it thickens; then add the yolks of three eggs beaten with two large tablespoonfuls sugar, and stir until much thicker than soft custard, and when somewhat cooled, add one teaspoonful vanilla, and pour it into a glass dish. Just before serving (when it must be perfectly cold), cover it with a meringue made of the whites of the eggs beaten stiff, with four tablespoonfuls sugar.

No. 112—CHOCOLATE BLANC-MANGE. —

Make exactly as in recipe No. 109, with the addition of four heaping tablespoonfuls grated chocolate rubbed smooth in a little milk; this is to be added as soon as the gelatine is perfectly dissolved.

No. 113—CORN STARCH BLANC-MANGE.

Heat one quart milk to boiling, then stir in four table-spoonfuls corn starch wet in a little cold water, with one saltspoon salt; boil five minutes, then add one small cup sugar, beaten with the yolk, of three eggs; boil two min-utes longer, stirring all the while; take from the fire and stir in the whites. Wet the mould with cold water. Many people prefer this without the eggs. Farina blanc-mange may be made in the same way, but boiled fifteen minutes instead of five before the eggs are added.

No. 114—Tapioca Blanc-Mange.

Soak one-half pound tapioca in a cup of cold water for four hours. Heat one pint rich milk and stir the tapioca into it. When it is quite dissolved, add three-quarters of a cup sugar and a pinch of salt. Boil slowly fifteen minutes, stirring all the time; take from the fire and beat till nearly cold, then add two teaspoonfuls of vanilla or bitter almonds, and pour into a mould dipped in cold water.

No. 115—Chocolate Cream.

Mix together according to previous directions two ounces chocolate, three eggs, a quarter of a pound sugar and a pint of milk. Stir over boiling water until smooth and creamy. Toast slices of any light, common cake, and pour the hot cream over them.

"We'll take the corn-starch blanc-mange for to-morrow," said Aunt Jane, "but we must find something for to-day's dessert. What shall it be?"

"Tip-top pudding," said Grace; "such as Rhoda makes."

"Can't we have our Queen of Puddings, mamma?" said Amy.

"You extravagant little things! You want nothing, but the richest and most delicate dishes that can be got up! I'm disposed to try something plain to-day. But I'll give you the receipts for the others too."

No. 116—Tip-Top Pudding.

Five oz. coffee sugar, one of butter, one quart milk, one pint stale bread crumbs, one lemon, four eggs. Grate the lemon rind and crumb the bread; beat the yolks of the eggs in the pudding dish; add gradually the sugar, lemon rind and butter rubbed to a cream; then the milk and bread alternately. Bake in a slow oven until firm. Beat the whites to a stiff froth with four tablespoonfuls powdered sugar, and enough of the lemon juice to flavor; spread this over the top and brown in the upper part of the oven. To be eaten hot or cold.

No. 117—Queen of Puddings.

One and a half cups sugar, two of fine bread crumbs, five eggs, one tablespoonful butter, one quart rich milk, one half cup jelly or jam, flavoring to taste. Rub the butter into one cup of the sugar; add the yolks beaten very light, and stir to a cream; next the bread crumbs, previously soaked in the milk, lastly the flavoring. Bake in a buttered pudding dish until "set," then draw to the front of the oven, cover first with jelly or jam, then with a meringue made of the whites whipped with the half cup of sugar.

Bake only to a very light brown.

No. 118—Bread Pudding.

One quart milk, two quarts bread crumbs, four eggs, beaten separately, two tablespoonfuls softened butter, one of white sugar, a little nutmeg, a quarter of a teaspoonful soda. Soak the crumbs well in the milk, add the yolks, well beaten, then the butter, seasoning and soda, lastly the whites. Eat with sweet sauce. A cupful of currants or raisins makes a very nice fruit pudding of this.

No. 119—Bread and Butter Pudding.

Four eggs, three cups milk, three-quarters of a cup sugar, one teaspoonful lemon or vanilla, a little nutmeg, some stale bread and butter. To be eaten cold.

"I should like to try that," said Grace. "Can we?"

"If Rhoda has any bread stale enough. We must look and see. Oh, yes, here is some that will do perfectly.

Cut this piece of a loaf into thin slices, Grace, and then spread them thickly with butter. Amy, you may make a custard of the rest of the materials, and Mabel can go to work on her farina blanc-mange."

When the pudding materials were prepared, a round baking dish was selected, into which the slices of bread and butter were neatly fitted, being cut to shape; each layer was sprinkled with sugar until the dish was half full. Then a small-sized, heavy plate was turned down over them to prevent them from floating, and the hot custard (for it had, of course, been made with scalded milk), was poured over them. After soaking for fifteen minutes the plate was taken off and the dish placed in the oven.

"You see the bread stays down very nicely to-day," said Mrs. King. "If it had risen to the top so as to threaten to make a hard crust, then we should have had to lay a silver tablespoon on it to keep it down until the custard was 'set,' as it is said to be as soon as it loses its liquid quality. By the way, I ought to have told you in giving you the recipe, that you can vary this delightfully by spreading the slices of bread and butter with jam or jelly instead of sugar; and also, that any kind of bread pudding is at least as good boiled as baked—*I* think better.

"How do you boil puddings, Aunt Jane?"

"If they are liquid you must boil them in a tin form; but for any kind of dough or paste puddings a square of heavy unbleached shirting is the best thing that ever was contrived. It must first be wrung out of boiling water, then well floured on the inside, then the edges gathered together and tied with a strong string, leaving a little room for the pudding or dumplings to 'swell' in."

"I wish we could make a dumpling," said Grace. "We haven't had one in a long time."

"We will, the first time we come in to cook in the morning. Not to-morrow, because we shall have Mabel's blanc-mange for dessert. How are you getting on, Mabel?"

"Pretty well, I think. Is'nt it thick enough now?"

"Yes, I think it is. Don't forget to wet the inside of your moulds with cold water."

While the bread and butter was soaking in custard, the other girls had been preparing the materials for some light cakes, for which Mrs. King had given them the recipes.

No. 120—EMILY'S CAKE.

One cup sugar, one-half cup butter, three eggs, half a

cup sweet milk, one teaspoonful cream tartar, one-half
soda, two and a half cups flour. Bake in jelly-cake
and fill with jelly or chocolate.

No. 121—CORN STARCH CAKE.

One cup butter, rubbed to a cream, with two of su
three eggs beaten separately, one cup milk, one teasp
soda, two cups of flour and half a cup corn sta
sifted together with two teaspoons cream tartar.

"Now I think of it," said Aunt Jane, after giv
them the last, "this will not do for to-day, as our din
is late and we shan't need any cake for tea. It is
nice when it is fresh, but ought to be eaten the same
or at least within twenty-four hours. Here are some
little things that will keep a long time."

No. 122—SUGAR CAKES.

One heaping teacup sugar, three quarters of a
butter, one quarter do. sweet milk, two well-beaten eg
two teaspoons cream tartar and one of soda, one s
spoon salt, spice to taste, flour enough to roll out. B
quickly in a hot oven.

"I have seen mamma put eggs into one side of

scales and sugar into the other," said Grace. "What was that for?"

"Oh, that's old-fashioned sponge-cake. Hardly any one makes it so now, but it can't be denied that it is the most elegant and exact way, and can *not* fail if your materials are good and your oven just right. You may as well write it down."

No. 123—NE PLUS ULTRA SPONGE CAKE.

Ten eggs, their weight in flour, half their weight in sugar, juice and rind of a lemon.

"Why is that any better than weighing things by the pound, Aunt Jane?"

"On account of the difference in the size of eggs. If they happen to be small, your cake may be rather plain; if they are uncommonly large it will be stiff and *eggy*. Using them as a measure of weight keeps every thing in its due proportion."

"I should like to try it some time, just for fun," said Grace.

"So you shall. Of course the eggs are beaten separately, and very light; the sugar goes with the yolks *after* they are thoroughly beaten, and is beaten again with them;

then beat in the lemon juice and peel, next the si
flour, and last of all the stiff whites. After they go
beat just enough to mix them, and bake immediate

Rhoda did not get back until rather late, and was
pleased to find her dessert already prepared. " I
thinking I'd have to put you off with a minute pudd
or some Jenny Linds," said she.

" Oh, what are they? give us the receipts!" cried Gr
pulling out her note book and writing down

No. 124—MINUTE PUDDING.

Boil a pint of milk with half a teaspoonful of salt.
soon as the milk begins to rise, stir in one pint of flc
When it is thoroughly mixed it is ready to serve.

" But the best part of it is the sauce," said Rhoda.

No. 125—LEMON SAUCE.

One large cup sugar and small half cup butter crean
together, one well-beaten egg stirred in, all the juice
half the grated peel of a lemon, a small teaspoonful n
meg; beat hard ten minutes, and add three tablespo
fuls boiling water, one at a time. Heat the sauce o
steam, but don't boil it.

"You have to make the sauce first, and then keep it hot over the steam of the tea-kettle," said Rhoda, "'cause the pudding must be served the minute it's done."

"Now for the Jenny Linds," said Grace.

No. 126—JENNY LINDS.

One tumblerful milk and the same of flour, half a teaspoonful salt and one egg. When the egg is well beaten stir in half the milk, then salt and flour, and beat all together; then add the rest of the milk. Bake in patty-pans and serve with

No. 127—JELLY SAUCE.

Half a cup currant jelly, two tablespoonfuls melted butter, the juice and half the grated peel of a lemon, half a teaspoonful nutmeg, one tablespoonful powdered sugar, two glasses wine. Beat the jelly to a smooth batter, then add gradually the butter, lemon and nutmeg; beat hard, then add sugar, and lastly wine. Keep warm, and also well covered, to prevent the escape of the flavor.

"That's very rich sauce," observed Amy.

"Yes, too rich for frequent use. When we make dumplings I'll give you the receipts for some plainer ones."

TENTH DAY.

"We are going to have company to tea to-morrow evening," said Mrs. Vernon one morning. "Have you girls a mind to get us up something nice?"

"Yes, indeed, Mamma. What shall we make?"

"I wish you'd let me be company, too, and not know anything about what we are going to have until I see it on the table. What do you say to that, Jane?"

"I should enjoy it. You give us *carte blanche*, of course?"

"Certainly. Do whatever you please, and send for whatever you want. You can't go amiss."

Thereupon Mrs. King and the young people withdrew to hold a private consultation.

"Let's have some new things, Aunt Jane," said Grace. "Something different from what Rhoda makes."

"I thought we would have some huckleberry cake," answered Aunt Jane; "but I suppose Rhoda knows all about that."

"Oh, no, I don't believe she does, for we never have it. It sounds excellent."

"Then there's a particularly nice kind of tea-cake that I know of, and that I don't believe your mother has the receipt for. And then you ought to know how to make old-fashioned pound cake."

"Oh, we're always having pound-cake! I can't bear it! Please let us put that off till some other day, and give us something new."

"So be it, then, but I'll give you the recipe while I think of it. That won't hurt you, at all events."

No. 128—POUND CAKE.

One pound sugar, one of flour, one of eggs, one of butter. Many people use but three-quarters of a pound of butter, and some add a glass of brandy. Beat *immensely*, and bake with care, not disturbing it after it is once set in the oven, or it will almost certainly be heavy.

No. 129—COMPANY TEA CAKE.

One quart flour and one of milk rubbed smoothly together; stir in six eggs beaten very light, and two-thirds of a cup softened butter. To be eaten hot, with butter.

No. 130—HUCKLEBERRY CAKE.

Two quarts flour, four tablespoons sugar, one very heaping tablespoonful butter, one teaspoon soda, two of cream tartar, milk enough to make a very thick batter. One quart berries. May be baked in muffin-rings, or in square flat tins. To be eaten hot, with butter.

No. 131—WASHINGTON CAKE.

Three cups of sugar, two of butter, one of milk, four of flour, five eggs, one teaspoonful soda and two of cream tartar. Mix as usual for other cake, then add half a pound currants and a quarter of pound raisins, both thoroughly floured. Some citron, finely sliced (my recipe says a handful,) and a little spice.

"What kind of spice, aunty?"

"Cinnamon and nutmeg are the most common, but I like a little allspice quite as well, especially where there is fruit. And you must all remember, when you come to bake cake by yourselves, that fruit cake requires a much longer time than the same recipe would need without it."

"Why does the fruit have to be floured?" asked Mabel.

"It will all sink to the bottom of the cake if it isn't," replied Mrs. King. "And even when it is carefully dredged, it will sometimes have a strong inclination to fall, especially if the batter is at all too thin, or the oven too slow. It requires care and judgment to bake fruit cake well. One great thing is to keep the heat perfectly even. Here is one you can try next winter, but I should advise you to make only half the receipt for the first time."

"Oh, I know what that means," said Grace, tossing her head. "You think we're going to spoil it."

"I think it is just as well to be careful, and that it would be a pity to waste those good nuts. But here's the recipe."

No. 132—NUT-CAKE.

Two cups sugar, one of butter, three of flour, one of cold water, four eggs, one teaspoonful soda and two of cream tartar, two cupfuls hickory nut kernels carefully picked out, without any teeth-breaking scraps of shell left among them.

"Why don't some of these receipts say baking-powder?" asked Mabel. "Rhoda always keeps it in the kitchen."

10

" Because the most particular cooks think tha
combination of soda and cream tartar is nicer
you ever happen to be without one of·these and
ing-powder, you may use as much of it as are r
the other two put together, or perhaps rather
you will be about right.   Here is a nice recipe
loaf-cake."

No. 133—Bread Cake.

One pound risen dough, half a pound sugar,
of a pound butter, half a tumblerful currants,
beaten egg, half a nutmeg, the grated rind and
juice of a lemon.   Mix thoroughly with the
set to rise.   Leave it in a warm place for seve
and do not bake until light.   It is better if bak
small loaves than in one large one.   Don't forg
ter the tins well.   It is not necessary to line t
paper.

" How are we to make the dough, Aunt Jane
" You will have to depend on Rhoda for tha
you are two or three years older, you can l
to use yeast; but at present we will confine our

to simple cooking. But I don't think you've had my favorite muffins yet."

No. 134—INDIAN-MEAL MUFFINS.

Two cups corn-meal, one of flour, two and a half of milk, three eggs, one tablespoonful lard, two of white sugar, one teaspoonful soda, two of cream tartar, one of salt. Beat whites and yolks separately, melt the lard, sift soda and cream tartar together with the flour (which must be added last of all,) and then beat with all your might. Bake in small patty-pans.

No. 135—GRAHAM BISCUIT.

Three cups Graham flour, one of white flour, three of milk, one tablespoonful lard, one well heaped of white sugar, one salt-spoon salt, one teaspoonful soda and two of cream tartar. Mix as for soda buscuit (No. 104).

"We might have some Sally Lunns, Mamma," said Amy. "They're good."

"Yes, but really Sally Lunns are made with yeast, and the modern imitations are not quite the same thing. Our 'company tea-cake' (No. 129) is not very different; but I'll give you the recipe."

No. 136—SALLY LUNNS.

One scant quart flour, one cup milk, half a
and the same of butter, four eggs, one teaspo
one of cream tartar and half as much soda. E
beaten separately; shortening melted; cream ta
into the flour, and soda dissolved in hot water,

No. 137—LAPLANDERS.

One pint Graham flour, one pint warm water,
beaten egg, half a teaspoonful salt. Beat the
one or two spoonfuls of the water, add the salt,
water, and the flour; beat thoroughly, then st
rest of the water. Have gem-pans very hot; but
and set immediately into the oven. To have
perfection, the small tins, after being heated
tered, should be set into a hot dripping-pan on t
the stove, and the batter poured in from a pitc
there may be no possibility of cooling. Made w
instead of water, these may be called Graham pu

"Why is it called Graham flour, Aunt Jane?"
"Because it was brought into general use
country by Dr. Graham, who thought fine flour e

unwholesome for everybody, and would have been glad to abolish it entirely if he could. It is not quite such a favorite now as it was once, but still everyone allows that it is more wholesome than fine flour, and it makes a pleasant variety for our table. Brown bread is made with yeast, like white."

"Have you decided yet what we shall have for tea, Aunt Jane?"

"We'll have huckleberry cake, certainly; and I was going to have tea-cake, but I think some biscuit and waffles will be best. You all want to get through in time to be dressed for tea, so we'll contrive not to have you too late in the kitchen. The biscuits may be put in to bake an hour beforehand, as it will not hurt them to stand half an hour if they are kept in a warm place; and, before you make them, you may mix the batter for the huckleberry cake, all but the soda, which Rhoda will add the last thing, and the same with the waffles, which, of course, she will have to bake. Some time when we have only our own family, I should like to have you learn to finish them entirely."

"We have no recipes for waffles, aunty."

"You shall have, if you will get out your note-books.

I'll give you three from Mrs. Miller's book, all delicious, as I can testify."

No. 138—BUFFALO WAFFLES.

One pound flour, two ounces butter, one quart milk, one gill of rice boiled in three of water, two even tablespoonfuls baking powder, two teaspoonfuls salt, two tablespoonfuls corn meal, four eggs. Melt the butter in the hot rice; sift the flour and powder together; beat the eggs very light, and pour in half of the milk, the flour, salt and rice; beat thoroughly, and by degrees add the other pint of milk, which should not be more than lukewarm. In baking, be careful to leave room in the iron for rising.

"Next comes a recipe for waffles without yeast or soda, which I shall take the liberty of re-christening."

No. 139—GENEVA WAFFLES.

One pint of milk, one pint one and a half gills of flour, two oz. of butter, three eggs, half a teaspoonful of salt. Melt the butter in the milk, and when sufficiently cooled mix it with the flour and salt; beat the whites and yolks separately, stir the yolks in the batter, and then the whites, very lightly.

No. 140—BARBY'S WAFFLES.

One and a half lbs. of flour, one pint or less of boiled rice, two and a half pints of sweet, rich milk, one teaspoonful of salt, four eggs. Put the rice in a four-quart bowl, separating the eggs, putting the yolks with the rice; add the salt, flour, and two pints of the milk, beating very thoroughly, then the remaining half pint of milk; beat the whites of the eggs to a stiff froth, add them to the batter, and beat well together. When thoroughly beaten, make the batter still lighter by lifting and pouring it with a tin cup for five minutes.

"Which of these shall we try, aunty?"

"The second, I think, although I should prefer either of the others, but we want something very simple, that will not detain you late in the kitchen. We haven't thought of any sweet-cake yet."

"Let's have some with fruit in," said Mabel, "because I like to stone the raisins."

"Here is a very nice recipe for that, and one that ought to · made to-day, because it wouldn't cut in nice slices if we put it off till to-morrow. Then in the morning we can make some jumbles so as to have a little variety; besides which, some people are afraid of fruit cake."

No. 141—AURORA CAKE.

Eleven oz. butter, one and a half pints sugar, two
a half pints flour, half a pint milk, one gill mixed w
and brandy, one and a half lbs. stoned raisins, a qua
of a teaspoonful baking powder sifted with the flour,
eggs. Cream the butter, add the sugar and yolks
beat until very light; stir in the milk, add alternately
whites beaten to a dry froth, and the flour, then the wi
and lastly the fruit; bake in deep pans, buttered, and li
with paper.

"There's some business for you, Mabel; it will take
a long time to find all the seeds in a pound and a half
raisins.   In the mean time, the rest of us will be gett
the other ingredients ready."

By tea-time the next evening, three nicely dressed c
dren were ready to take their places at the table;
when the visitors learned that the fresh tea-biscuit,
waffles and huckleberry cake, the rich, delicate jumb
and fine fruit cake, were the work of those little han
they could scarcely believe their ears.

"But we had to have help with the baking, you kno
said Grace, who was too honest to take more praise t
she deserved. "You musn't give us credit for that."

"That will all come in time," answered Mrs. Brown, "and I should be very proud if my little girls could make as nice things as those, even if somebody else did bake them."

ELEVENTH DAY.

"It is a drizzling, chilly, forlorn kind of day, Aunt Jane; don't you think it would be a good time to have a dumpling?"

"Excellent; I know you've been wanting to try your hand at that, Gracie, for a long time. We'll not only make a dumpling, but we'll write down all kinds of winter recipes that you can make by yourselves on Saturday mornings, if your lessons haven't tired you too much during the week."

"Oh, I know we shall want to; see if we don't! And at any rate, we shall want to know how, whether we do it or not."

"But you will soon find out that to do it well you must keep in practice. It is just like playing the piano, or drawing, in that respect. You will soon lose your skill if you don't exercise it."

"But we have made all our plans for a regular cooking-club, and we *can't* forget. We'll write you about it, and tell you the nice things we make."

"That will be the next thing to eating them," said Aunt Jane. "I know a good many ladies who really enjoy sitting down and poring over a cookery book, though they haven't the least intention of making the things. I shall take a great deal of pleasure in thinking of the nice desserts and tea-dishes and lunches you make."

"Who's going to cook to-day, Aunt Jane?"

"Only the older girls. Boiled dough of all sorts belongs to the department of pastry, and that, you know, the little ones haven't begun upon yet. So if you don't mind the rain, you may go for Rose and Edith.'

"Papa says that people who are afraid of rain must be made of either sugar or salt, and think they are going to melt. So as I seem to be composed of pretty solid flesh, I think I'll go."

It didn't take long to collect the party, who had been groaning a little over being obliged to spend the day indoors, and were glad of something to do.

Aunt Jane received them in the parlor, where they were to write their recipes. She had in her hand a very old-looking brown book, which when opened showed pages yellow with age, covered with fine manuscript in faded ink.

"Oh, what's that, Aunt Jane?" asked Grace.

"My mother's old, old receipt-book, that I rem
ever since I was a little child. It must have been
at least fifty years ago, as I see her maiden nam
and added to, year by year, for a great many years.
mother surprised me by bringing it out this mo
when I thought it had long ago passed over to the '
that were.'"

"Are we going to make any of the things in it?

"Not to-day, perhaps, but you may write dowi
of the directions if you want to, and try them som
by yourselves. Here is one of the very oldest."

No. 142—A Cheese-Cake.

Four eggs, half a gill milk, a quarter of a poun
ter, the same of powdered sugar, two ounces grated
two tablespoonsful brandy and the same of wine,
spoonful of rose-water, the same of mixed mace,
mon and nutmeg, a quarter of a pound currants.
pare puff paste first; have the currants very clean a
serve some for sprinkling over the cheese-cake; sp
the remainder with flour; stir the butter and sug
cream; grate the bread and prepare the spice; be

eggs very light; boil the milk and then add to it half the eggs (beaten together) and boil the mixture till it becomes a curd, stirring frequently with a knife; then mix in the bread, and afterward stir all together, including the currants, into the butter and sugar; then add the remaining half of the egg, and by degrees the liquor and spice. Line patty-pans or pie dishes with puff paste, fill with the mixture, sprinkling the reserved currants over the top; then bake.

"What an elaborate receipt!" exclaimed Rose.

"Not more so than some we have made. It is because the directions are so very full that it seems long. It is an old English recipe, and a real English housekeeper never cares how much time she spends on any thing that is to be very nice. Here we like to get through everything as fast as possible, and use our time for something else."

"I have often read about cheese-cakes in English stories," said Edith, "such as Miss Edgeworth's and Mrs. Barbauld's, and the children always seemed to think them a great treat."

"Here is another recipe, which seems very much like our modern 'floating island.'"

No. 143—A Good Cream.

To one quart of boiled milk add the yolks of six eggs well beaten up with four tablespoonfuls white sugar; (if not sweet enough for your taste you can add more sugar;) let the milk stand a few minutes before you put in the eggs. Beat the whites of the eggs to a froth and then stir them in the hot cream; they will rise to the top and then may be taken off and drained, and after your cream is dished you can put the froth on the top. You boil whatever flavor you choose in the milk, and call your cream after the flavor.

" That's simple enough, any way," said Rose.

" Yes, it's very simple, but I think our taste now-a-days requires that the eggs and milk should be thickened together by a little boiling. But here's something I know you never saw."

No. 144—Gingerbread–Nuts.

Two pounds flour, one of butter, half a pound brown sugar, one quart sugar-house molasses, two ounces ginger, one teaspoonful allspice, one of cinnamon, and the same of cloves. Cut up the butter in the flour, crush the sugar

fine with the rolling pin, mix it with the flour, and afterward add the spice and molasses. Flour your pie-board
and take the dough, a large handful at a time, and knead
it in separate cakes; then knead all very hard together
for a long time. Cut the lump in halves, roll it out in
two even sheets about half an inch thick, and cut in little
cakes the size of a cent. Bake on buttered tins in a very
moderate oven, as gingerbread is more apt to scorch than
any other cake.

"Why, what mites of cakes, Mrs. King," said Edith.
"Hardly larger than a thimble."

"Oh, they didn't have nickel cents in those days,"
replied Mrs. King. "This means an old-fashioned cop-
per cent, more like the top of this little canister in size.
I remember the gingerbread-nuts perfectly, and very
good they were; but it required a world of patience to
make them. Another way, and one I liked better, was to
roll them into little balls like marbles. Here is a recipe
that I used to think very good. I don't know how I
should like it now."

No. 145—Honey Cake.

Four cups flour, four eggs, two cups honey, one teaspoonful pearlash, nutmeg or cinnamon to taste.

"What is pearlash, Aunt Jane?"

"A kind of alkali formerly used in cooking, whie afterward supplanted by saleratus, and now by Pearlash is a refined preparation of potash, which is from wood ashes."

"Then it must be what they make soap with, Grace.

"Yes, the same thing. Lye is an alkali in a form. From this dear old receipt-book I can give direction for making soap, if you like—both har soft."

"Thank you, my dear aunt, we won't trouble y long as we can buy it ready-made. Perhaps if v ever cast away on a desert island and have nothi wash with, we may be glad to have the receipt."

"Now it is time to think of our dumpling," said Jane.

No. 146—CRUST FOR DUMPLINGS. ——

Two cups milk, one heaping tablespoonful lard an same of butter, one teaspoonful soda and two of c tartar, one salt-spoon salt, flour enough to make a dough. Some people prefer it made with two well-

en eggs to a pound of flour, mixed with water enough
to make a dough; the other ingredients the same.

No. 147—Suet Paste.

Rub well with half a pound finely chopped beef suet,
three-quarters of a pound flour, and one saltspoon salt;
make into a paste with cold water, work it well, beat it
with the rolling-pin, and roll it out two or three times.
This paste answers for any kind of boiled fruit pudding.

No. 148—Potato Paste.

Mash one pound boiled potatoes, while still warm, and
rub into them with the hands three-quarters of a pound
flour and half a teaspoonful salt; make it into a stiff
paste with cold water; beat and roll as above. Especially nice for roller dumplings.

"What are they, Aunt Jane?"
"You may as well write down the recipe."

No. 149—Roller Dumplings.

Take any of the above kinds of paste and roll out very
thin. Then spread it evenly to within half an inch of the
edge with any kind of jam or similar preserve (not

11

liquid), then begin with the side next you and roll up carefully to the shape of a bolster. The farther edge should be left uncovered for an inch, and the edges wet all round that they may adhere to each other. Then take a piece of stout cloth of the same shape as the roll, but larger, roll the dumpling in it, and tie up the ends, first dipping the cloth in hot water, wringing it out and flouring the inside.

"Then you boil it, I suppose," said Edith.

"Oh, yes, that is always understood of a dumpling, though I have seen a recipe for a baked one. I never tried it, but I have it here, and you may copy it if you choose."

No. 150—Baked Apple Dumplings.

Prepare a regular "dumpling-crust"; roll it out, cut into squares and in the center of each lay a juicy, tart apple, pared and cored; bring the corners of the square neatly together and pinch them slightly. Lay in a buttered baking pan, the joined edges downward, and bake to a fine brown. When done, brush over with beaten egg and set back into the oven to glaze for a few minutes. Sift powdered sugar over them and eat with sauce.

No. 151—To glaze Pastry.

The appropriate glazing for meat pies is made with beaten yolk of egg alone, laid on with a feather or paste-brush; for a lighter color (like that for the baked dumplings), the whole of the egg may be beaten together. The best method of glazing fruit tarts before they are sent to the oven is to moisten the paste with ice-water, sift sugar thickly upon it, and press it lightly with the hand; but when a whiter icing is preferred, the pastry must be drawn from the oven when nearly baked and brushed with white of egg whisked to a froth, then well covered with the sifted sugar and sprinkled with a few drops of water before it is put in again.

No. 152—Flaky Paste.

After mixing together as for puff paste (No. 64), and giving the first application of butter, brush over with whipped white of egg before you fold it to roll out again. Repeat this process each time, or four times in all.

"That has nothing to do with dumplings, has it, Aunt Jane?"

"No, but I was reminded of it by the directions for

glazing. It does not make the paste taste any better; if anything, it will not be quite as tender, but it will flake very elegantly, and is handsome when you are preparing for company."

No. 153— BAKING POWDER BISCUIT.

One lb. flour, one tablespoonful butter and two of lard, three-quarters of a pint sweet milk, one even teaspoonful salt and five of baking powder, sifted with the flour; rub the shortening through with the hand until quite fine, pour in the milk, mix lightly, and roll out on a floured board without any kneading, cut with a round cutter, and bake in a quick oven.

"What do you give us biscuit now for, Aunt Jane?"

"Because the very same recipe makes capital dumpling-paste, and I want to give you your choice. Now we come to what we shall have to-day—peach dumpling."

"Oh, good! I didn't know we had any peaches."

"I think the fact has been carefully concealed from you because the peaches are not ripe enough to eat raw; they are rather hard and green, but they will do very well for a pie."

No. 154—Peach Dumpling.

Make a paste by any of the above recipes; roll it out to half an inch thickness, pile as many cut-up peaches on it as you think the paste will cover, mixing through them a tablespoonful of coffee sugar; gather the edges of the paste carefully together, so as to make the dumpling as nearly as possible a round ball; tie it in a well-floured cloth wrung out of hot water; turn a plate upside down in the kettle to prevent the cloth from sticking to it; plunge the dumpling into boiling water and boil two hours.

"Now we will go down to the kitchen," said Aunt Jane, "and while Grace is making the paste, Rose and Edith, between them, can make some cake for tea."

"Shall I go into the cellar to make it, Aunt Jane?" asked Grace.

"Oh no, that is not necessary for boiled paste, or dough, as some people call it, though dough is properly only what is raised with yeast. It will be just as nice made here, and it is more sociable for us to be all together. Make your paste from the first recipe—simple 'dumpling crust.' Now, Rose, as we have had nothing here for a long time but fine cake, you may make some ginger cup-cakes, after one of these old recipes."

No. 155—Molasses Cup-Cakes.

Two cups molasses, two of brown sugar rolled fine, one of rich milk, one of butter, five of sifted flour, five eggs, one heaping tablespoonful ginger, one teaspoonful allspice and one of cloves. Bake in small tins in a moderate oven. If not spiced enough for the taste, add more ginger.

"Why do they so often speak of 'rich milk,' Aunty?"

"I suppose because some people use skimmed milk for cooking, after taking off the cream for coffee, and the person who writes the recipe doesn't want to have the article spoiled. Never use skim-milk in cooking, if you can get any other. Oh, I forgot that the peaches were not prepared yet; you two girls may pare and cut them up while Gracie is making the paste, and afterwards she will help you to prepare your materials."

"Does this paste look about right, Aunt Jane?" asked Grace when she had rolled it out.

"Yes, just right; now we must have a two-quart tin pan or a round vegetable-dish to lay it in to keep the peaches in place. If Rhoda will wring the cloth out of hot water for you, you can rub it inside with flour, then lay it in the dish, put in your paste and afterward the peaches and sugar which the girls have been getting ready for you, and then all you have to do is to gather the edges together and press them tightly so that no water can get inside.   Now we will tie up the cloth, not too close to the ball, because there must be a little room left for it to swell in, nor too loosely, because that would let it fall out of shape; but just—so!"

"I quite long for dinner-time to come," said Grace. "Not so much because I want to taste it myself as to see how the rest like it, especially mamma and papa."

"You may make your mind perfectly easy about that, Grace; I *know* it will be good."

"Are apple dumplings made in the same way?"

"Yes; and so are cherry and blackberry and huckleberry, and any thing else you like to use.   Many people make all these things into what they call 'bolsters,' or rollers, but I dont think they are nearly as nice as when the fruit is all kept together in the middle."

"What a queer name for anything to eat — bolsters!"

"I don't think it's an agreeable one, so I never call them so.   Sometimes they are called 'valise puddings,' which isn't so bad, but that there isn't anything in the valises used **now-a-days (which are shaped like little trunks,)** to remind **you of them."**

" What kind **of sauce must we have for this?"**

" At home **we always had them served in this way: a** plate of butter **was set by the one who served the dump-** lings, and a piece **of it was placed directly in the mid-** dle of each **helping; this was covered with a great** spoonful of **white sugar and the eater distributed them** for himself, so **we'll have it done in that way to-day, to** remind your mother **of old times."**

" But I suppose **some people eat sauce with it, don't** they?" inquired **Rose.**

" Yes; generally **hard sauce, though liquid sauce is** equally admissible."

" How do **you make hard sauce, Aunt Jane?"**

" Why, did **I never tell you?   Then you must have the** recipe for it straightway."

No. 156—HARD SAUCE.

Beat to a **cream one cup butter, to which add three** cups powdered **sugar.   Beat long and hard, then place** upon a small **dish and smooth into shape with a knife-** blade dipped in **cold water.   It is made richer by having** half a cup of wine, or the juice of a lemon, or both, beaten up with it. When smooth, grate nutmeg thickly on the top.

"Here is another extremely nice one:"

No. 157—FRUIT PUDDING SAUCE.

Half a cup of butter, two and a half cups sugar, one cup boiling water, one dessert spoonful corn starch wet with a little cold milk, one glass of wine, the juice and half the peel of a lemon. Cream the butter and sugar together; pour the corn starch into the boiling water and stir until well thickened; beat all together five minutes in a bowl off the fire, heat then until nearly boiling, add the wine and serve.

No. 158—FRENCH SAUCE.

Beat half a pound butter to a cream, stir in half a pound brown sugar, add the beaten yolk of an egg and one gill of wine, place it over the fire and keep stirring till it simmers. Grate nutmeg over it before it is sent to table.

"That is an excellent sauce for apple dumplings," observed Aunt Jane, "but I can tell you of one much

simpler — plain molasses. I think the combinati
excellent."

"Isn't it for other dumplings too, Mrs. King?" inq
Edith.

"No; with any other fruit the molasses seems t(
stroy the delicacy of the flavor; but it just suits
apple."

"I should like to make some little apple dumpli
said Rose, "such as the farmer's wife gave King G(
the Third, and he couldn't possibly imagine how the
ple got in there."

"He wasn't the wisest of men, was he?" said
Jane. "But all you have to do is to roll out your
and cut little squares of it just large enough to cove
apple, then peel and core your apple, put a little sug
the hole in the center, wrap it tightly in the paste
drop it into boiling water. It doesn't need any cloth
cause it keeps its shape well enough without, that i
the paste is not too rich. Very particular people tie
one up in a separate square of cloth; but for a famil
the size of ours, when some at least will want a se
dumpling or part of one, it would be a great labor
think I should let them take their chance in a
large pot with a plate in the bottom of it."

"Have you come to the end of your dumpling recipes, Aunt Jane?"

"By no means, but we have about come to the end of our time, for Rhoda will want us to get out of the way so that she can cook the dinner. So we'll just get the cup-cakes into the oven, and leave the rest of our recipes until another time."

TWELFTH DAY.

"Mamma, did you know that Friday was Jessie's birth-day?" asked Grace, pursuing her mother into her bed-room and shutting the door cautiously. "It is, and Aunt Carroll says she will have a little party for her if we will go over and make the things; and won't you please in-vite Jessie here to spend Thursday with Mabel and Amy, so that we can have some surprises?"

"Don't you think Jessie will enjoy it more if she has the pleasure of anticipation too?" inquired Mrs. Vernon.

"Oh, she knows she is going to have company, but then we'd like to have just a few things that none of them know anything about; and if she is at home she'll want to be all the time in the kitchen, and she'll be in the way, and then the other girls will come over to see her, and so, you see——"

"And so, I see, you've settled it all among yourselves beforehand. Very well; I shall make no objection to any thing your aunts decide upon. I suppose Aunt Jane will superintend, as usual."

"We haven't asked her, but I know she will," said Grace, and ran off to make sure of it.

Any one who knows Aunt Jane can easily guess the answer. Soon after breakfast on Thursday morning she met the three older girls at Mrs. Carroll's.

"Mamma is just going to have a simple lunch to-day and a late dinner," said Rose, "so that nothing can possibly interfere with us, and we'll have the whole day to ourselves."

"Your mother and I have had some consultation about our refreshments and other matters," said Mrs. King. "At first we were going to have the good old-fashioned hours of four to eight, but there must be a birthday cake, and that wouldn't be any thing without candles, and the candles won't show by daylight; so, all things considered, as the weather is very hot and the visitors wouldn't want to come out early in the afternoon, the invitations have been made from five to nine."

"The three little ones are going round giving them this morning," said Rose.

"So we will have a regular tea (only there won't be any tea,) at half-past six; and about a quarter before nine we'll have the cake, all lighted up, and some lemonade."

The girls approved of this, and Aunt Jane set them at work without delay. "We'll get our fruit ready first of all," said she. "It is very tedious to stop after one has begun cooking to stone raisins or wash currants."

Grace and Edith took the dish of raisins between them, with a small case-knife apiece, a plate on which to put the seeded fruit, a bowl of water to dip their sticky fingers in, and a towel to wipe them on; also a piece of brown paper on which to scrape off the seeds.

"It is never any loss of time," said Mrs. King, "to make everything as convenient as possible before you begin. Make-shifts seem to save a minute or two at first, but they don't in the end."

Rose undertook to prepare the dried currants. "Oh, what dirty things!" she exclaimed. "Are *these* what they put in cake?"

"Just these and nothing else," answered Aunt Jane. "But after they have passed through your hands they will be quite another thing. Shake them out over this large dish, and pick out the most obvious intruders—stones, leaves, sticks, and so forth."

After this the currants were poured into a large pan of water, rinsed round, and allowed to settle. This was repeated four times, the water looking less and less black after each operation. After the fifth water was poured off, Mrs. King said they were ready to dry.

"Now take this large crash towel and rub them in it, a few at a time," said she.

It was surprising to see how much dirt and how many scraps of foreign matter the currants had contrived to retain in spite of all their duckings and sousings; but towels were plenty and Rose was almost nervously neat, and she did not let them go until they were what she called "really, truly, *eatably* clean."

"This fruit is all for the birthday cake," said Aunt Jane, as she showed her pupils how to shred up citron. "What we will have on the tea-table will be quite plain."

"What else are we going to have for tea?" asked Grace.

"First and foremost, cold boiled ham and cold tongue; those are the solids; then biscuit, jam puffs, chocolate, and, if you choose to make them, lemon jelly and soft custard."

"Of course we will!"

"Berries are so common everywhere, that I think the little girls would like the jelly better. We can have a handsome dish of oranges for the center of the table, so as not to be quite without fruit. Then of course, there must be several kinds of cake for the tea-table. We might have small sponge-cakes, crisp cookies, cocoanut drops and jumbles. How would you like to try some macaroons?"

"Splendid! We should like it ever so much! But we haven't any recipes for them."

"I've brought over my book on purpose, and you may write them down before we begin."

No. 159—Crisp Cookies.

One pound sugar, one of flour, one half-pound butter, half a nutmeg, or any other spice, five eggs.

No. 160—Macaroons.

The whites of three eggs beaten to a stiff froth, half a pound of powdered sugar, half a pound desiccated cocoanut, half a pint rolled and sifted crackers, one teaspoonful extract of bitter almond; drop them on buttered paper in a dripping-pan, and bake light brown.

No. 161—Small Sponge Cakes.

One teacup powdered sugar, one of flour, three eggs,

half a teaspoonful cream tartar, a quarter of a teaspoonful soda.

"How can we ever measure a quarter of a teaspoonful, Aunt Jane?"

"Measure your half one of cream tartar and divide it into two little piles; then make a pile of soda of the size of one of these. That isn't hard to do."

"And what will be the name of the birthday cake, Aunt Jane?'

"What I made for Amy's last birth-day was Dover cake, and I don't think there's anything nicer for the purpose. You have it in your receipt-books, number 34. To that we add a pound of raisins, a pound of currants, a quarter of a pound of citron, a glass of brandy and some spice, and that makes a fruit-cake of it. This recipe makes a very large loaf, which of course must be iced, so it will present quite an imposing appearance. Usually we bake it in two loaves, but to-day it must go into a four quart tin pan."

Mrs. King didn't have to tell the girls a word about putting the cake together that day, they had done it so often before. She watched them with great pleasure as one set about beating the whites of eggs, another the

12

yolks, and the third creamed the butter and afterwards beat up the sugar with it, then added the yolks of eggs, afterward the milk and soda, and finally the whites of eggs and flour alternately, a little of each at a time. The soda she directed them to mix in a very little vinegar, as that has a peculiar effect in producing lightness, especially in certain kinds of rich cake. There was only one thing Aunt Jane had to remind them of, and that was that they must save out some of the flour to rub the fruit in. If she hadn't done that, I do believe they would have put it all in, and then had to add more and so make the cake plainer, for it would never have done to put in the fruit without dredging.

When it had been beaten enough to satisfy even Aunt Jane's requiring eye, the three cooks taking it in turn, the light batter was poured into the tin pan, which had been lined with nice white paper and well buttered.

"We mus'nt make it a bit more than half full," said Aunt Jane, "for this is an aspiring cake, and he means to rise and rise till he fills the whole pan and rounds up in the middle in a little hill. Now the fire must be kept very even, and we shan't need to look at the cake for a long time, so as to give it a chance to get well set. Then it may want turning."

"I have a bright idea, girls," said Aunt Jane when the oven door had been closed upon the cake from which so much was expected. "Instead of soft custard, suppose we make whipped cream for to-morrow, as this is a great occasion."

"Oh, that would be perfectly delicious," cried Rose. "Everybody likes whipped cream, and it will look so much more like a party than custard, such as we have every few days. Is there any particular recipe for it, Aunt Jane?"

"Yes, indeed; I'll give it to you now, though we can't make the cream till to-morrow, because it must be fresh."

No. 162—Whipped Cream.

One pint cream, one small cup fine sugar, one gill wine. Mix all together in a large bowl and beat hard with a whisk, or what is still better, churn with a whip-churn. As the froth rises, take it carefully off with a spoon, and place in the dish in which it is to be served.

"That will look beautiful with the jelly," said Edith. "What kind shall we make to go with it?"

"We haven't tried orange jelly yet; and as there is to be wine in the cream, we don't care for wine jelly to eat

with it. I think orange will suit our young friends as well
as anything."

No. 163—ORANGE JELLY. ⸺

Juice of two oranges and grated rind of one, one lemon, juice and peel, one package Cox's gelatine, soaked in
a very little water for an hour, one pint boiling water,
one cup and a half sugar, half a cup of wine, a good pinch
of cinnamon.

"The gelatine has been soaking more than an hour,"
said Aunt Jane, "and we may as well begin on it now as
any time. Edith, you may make the jelly, Rose the
jumbles, and Grace the macaroons. While the jelly is
under way, Edith will have time to make the cocoanut
drops. All these will keep nicely if they are shut up
tight. To-morrow we will make the little sponge-cakes,
soda biscuits, puffs, chocolate and whip."

"I thought you said we would have crisp cookies, Aunt
Jane."

"Did I? I think we shall have quite enough without
them. We'll leave them until some other time. They
are exceedingly nice, are made without any soda, and will
keep a long time. Now get to work, all of you."

After Edith had grated the peel of the oranges and lemons, and squeezed out the juice very thoroughly, she threw in the cinnamon, and then poured on them a pint of boiling water. The whole was then closely covered, that the flavor might be completely diffused. Then, as it was to remain so for half an hour, Edith left it and made the cocoanut drops; after which the jelly-water was strained and the sugar stirred in. It was then put over the fire until it boiled, when the soaked gelatine was stirred in, and as soon as this was dissolved, the whole was poured into a flannel bag and run into moulds.

The cocoanut drops, being made after the following simple recipe, did not take a very long time.

No. 164—Cocoanut Wafers.

Half a pint powdered sugar, the same of desiccated cocoanut, three even tablespoonfuls of flour, half a teaspoonful vanilla, two eggs. Beat the eggs and add successively the sugar, vanilla, flour and cocoanut. Bake on buttered paper.

When the birth-day cake came out, after being inspected by many admiring eyes, it was set away in the pan to cool. "We must ice it over the top," said Aunt

Jane, " so as to keep this beautiful rounded side upper-most. A loaf that is to be cut in the pantry and not appear on the table except in slices, should be iced on the bottom, and then it is handsome all round. If you have ever noticed little pound cakes or anything of that sort, they are always iced in that way, and so look as if they had two tops, one white and one brown."

What do you suppose Grace and Aunt Jane found when they went home to tea that evening? That those rogues of little girls had persuaded their mother to let them go into the kitchen and make things all by themselves! Rhoda was out, and they had full liberty to do as they pleased, under the single condition of leaving everything in good order after them. There was a good fire, which one of the other servants attended to, and they had followed the devices of their own minds in what they did, each one selecting some easy-looking dish that did not require expensive materials. Mabel took a pint of milk and two eggs, which she beat up together with a great deal of fine sugar and vanilla, and made very good little custards of it, only rather strong and sweet. She also forgot to grate nutmeg over the top, which was not an important omission, however. Jessie made some No. 63

cup-cake, using the after-dinner coffee-cups for it, so as to make a small quantity, and two eggs instead of four. She found some difficulty in estimating half the quantity named of soda and cream tartar, but after much solemn consultation among the three, it was measured out, and the cake proved excellent, though a little broken on the under side, owing to the difficulty of getting it out, the tins not having been buttered. Amy had moused about till she found an old receipt-book of her aunt's, in which there were directions for " sugar drops," a confection not named in her mother's list; so she copied it into her book and made half the quantity, for fear they should not turn out well.

No. 165—Sugar Drops.

Beat the whites and yolks of four eggs separately to a light foam; dilute the yolks with two teaspoonfuls of water, add the whites and beat for some time together; then add by degrees a pound of fine powdered sugar, and afterward a quarter of a pound of flour, beating constantly. Flavor with extract of lemon or orange juice. Drop spoonfuls of the mixture on buttered paper, ice them over with powdered sugar, and bake about ten minutes.

These were, if anything, the crowning success of the
day. The only trouble was that the children found them
so good they had hard work to keep any to show what
they had been about; but finally Amy seized what remained and resolutely shut them up in the closet, "out
of the way of temptation," as she said, which gave the
impression that the sugar drops were in some mysterious
way tempted to be eaten.

The birth-day itself was a busy one at Aunt Carroll's.
First of all, there was the great cake to be iced. They
decided on a plain icing (No. 57), flavored with lemon,
and Mrs. King told them how it must be made.

"You must beat the whites of eggs only till they are a
little frothy before you begin to add the sugar," said she.
"Beating them stiff only increases the labor, and makes
the icing slow in drying and sticky when done. Shake
in the sugar slowly with your left hand while you beat
with the right. When you have cranberry sauce, it
makes a very pretty variety to color a part of the icing
with the jelly when you are icing small cakes. As I told
you, they are always iced on the bottom, and to keep
them firm while the icing is hardening, you can lay thin
strips of wood across the sieve just far enough apart to

rest the edges of the cake on and support it. A round loaf of cake will often fit into the top of a vegetable dish."

As soon as the cake was thickly iced, and before it was dry, Aunt Jane said she would show the girls what she once saw done by a professional cook. She had procured from the confectioner's some pink frosting-sugar, and had made a little horn of white paper with an opening at the small end about as large as the head of a pin. Then she traced very lightly with a pin-point on the icing a pretty border in a sort of embroidery pattern, and in the center the word "Jessie," with the date of the anniversary underneath it.

"Now, Rose," said she, "take this in your hand and go slowly over all the pattern I have traced on the top of the cake. The pink sugar will run out through the little hole in the end of the horn, and as the icing dries it will close in round it and keep it in place, even after it is cut. Not so fast! Your lines will be too thin; and not too slowly or you will make a heap instead of a fine line. There; now that your hand moves steadily it looks very pretty."

"It is too bad to spoil this handsome cake by sticking candles into it," said Edith.

" The same thing occurred to me," answered Mrs. King; " and besides, the wax is almost sure to run down on the icing, and then that has to be thrown away. I have seen one pretty good contrivance to prevent this. Each candle was set in a little flat candlestick, from the bottom of which projected downwards a sharp piece of tin which held it in the cake. That did very well, but I found something yesterday at a toy shop that I like still better."

Then she showed them ten little tall candlesticks which were to stand on the table immediately round the cake, and could be easily removed when the candles were burned down. The children still thought there ought to be one in the middle of the cake " to grow on," but at last decided to be contented without it.

After this chief ornament was finished, the girls turned their attention to the rest of the entertainment. There was plenty of icing left for the little sponge-cakes, which looked extremely pretty in the cake basket mixed with macaroons and cocoanut drops. The chocolate, being for young people, was diluted with double the quantity of milk given in ordinary recipes, and was quite as acceptable; the whipped cream and orange jelly made a very agreeable contrast in color, being served together in the same saucer; and as for the biscuit, made by Rose, and Grace's puffs, filled with different kinds of jelly, all that needs to be said of them is that they were worthy of Aunt Jane's Cooking Class.

THIRTEENTH DAY.

"I think of inviting some friends to lunch to-morrow, Jane," said Mrs. Vernon to her sister soon after the birthday party. "May we depend on you and the girls again?"

"With all my heart," answered Mrs. King. "Just tell us what you would like to have, and we'll do our best to please you, ma'am."

"I think you might better tell me what you would like to make," said Mrs. Vernon. "I'm very humble. I'd put up with anything—that was good."

"We musn't have any of the dishes we made for Aunt Carroll's lunch, because we want to try some novelties. Broiled chickens are good, but the girls are hardly old enough to undertake those, and I want that the cooking should be *bona fide* their own. What do you say to a dish of sweetbreads, a nice salad, and potato croquettes?"

"I can't imagine anything better; but do you know what you are undertaking?"

"Oh, yes, perfectly; you don't know how skillful the little things have become, now that they have their heart in the matter. All I do is to look at them; they would feel quite hurt if I touched anything."

"I am delighted to hear it. I had no idea that the fancy would hold out so long. What do you think would be nice in the way of sweets?"

"Peaches are tolerably plenty now, and I should like to show the girls some ways of using them. An open pie in puff paste would be very handsome."

"Elegant! Anything else?"

"A chocolate meringue makes a good variety, and we might have coffee instead of chocolate, so as not to have too much of the same thing, and some light cake, not very rich. Rolls are the best thing in the way of bread, but as they are out of our line, we will make some biscuit instead. And you must not forget that the children have the promise of setting the table, so we must do what we can to-day to give them more time."

"Arrange everything just as you please," said Mrs. Vernon; "I'm only too thankful to have it off my hands."

Then Mrs. King brought her little army together and explained the bill of fare to them. They found the prospect of getting up such a handsome lunch very exciting, and wanted to begin at once.

"We must ask Rhoda to have plenty of mashed potato ready for the croquettes," said Mrs. King, "and, I think, the peach pie and some jelly cake might be made to-day; I don't see what more we can do. Grace, you succeed very well with pastry; you may go directly into the cellar and make your handsomest puff-paste, and we'll prepare the fruit for you in the mean time."

Mabel then began to peel the peaches, while Mrs. King showed Amy how to make a new kind of cake for jelly.

No. 166—MARTHA'S CAKE.

Three eggs, one cup of sugar, one of flour, a piece of butter the size of an egg, one teaspoonful cream tartar, half a teaspoonful soda, dissolved in a tablespoonful milk.

"This is a very simple cake," said her mother, "and we may think when we come to look at it to-morrow that it is too plain for company; if so, we can make some of Jenny's nice sponge cake, from our No. 6 receipt. Here is another that you may write down."

No. 167—PUFF CAKE.

Two cups sugar, two and a half of flour, half a cup of butter, one of milk, three eggs, a teaspoonful cream tartar and half a teaspoonful soda.

While Amy put the cake together, Mrs. King and
Mabel pared, stoned and cut up the peaches. Then Mabel
weighed them, and found that there were two pounds.
These her aunt told her to put over the fire in a saucepan with one pound of white sugar and a cupful of water.
"We don't stew peaches for ordinary pies," said she,
"but as I want this one to look handsome as well as taste
nice, I am going to take extra pains with it."

When about half cooked the peaches were taken off the
fire and set away for awhile, and by the time Grace's
paste was ready to roll out, they were cool enough to use.
When a couple of pie-plates had been lined with paste,
the stewed peaches were poured into them until even
with the top; across this strips of paste were laid in dia-
mond-shaped lattice-work, each strip being twisted like a
strand of worsted cord before it was placed over the com-
pote; then a margin of paste just the size of that of the
pie-dish was laid on, the under surface being first wet
with cold water.

"Why did you stew these first, Aunt Jane?" asked
Grace.

"For several reasons. Unless the peaches had been
piled up high in the middle, which would have made the

surface uneven, they would have shrunken so much as to have made the top fall in; then they would have taken so much longer to cook than the paste, that it would have become quite brown by the time they were done. (By the way, I'll tell you how to make a beautiful apple-pie when we get through with this.) Now you will see that when the pie is cold there will be a smooth jellied surface, and you musn't forget to have some powdered sugar ready to sift over it the instant it comes out of the oven."

"Now tell me about the apple-pie, please."

No. 167—APPLE PIE.

Pare, core and slice very fine, ripe, tart apples; place a layer in the bottom of a pie-dish, then a layer of sugar, over which sprinkle the smallest pinch of ground cloves; repeat this process until the dish is full, pour in a tablespoonful of water, cover with puff-paste not rolled out very thin, and bake. This is far more healthful than pies baked with an under-crust, though the same recipe will answer for that kind also.

The next morning Rose came in saying that her mamma would like to have her wait on the table with the other girls, if agreeable to Aunt Nelly, and offering her services as cook. At the same time Mabel was invited to spend the morning with Jessie, with the promise that she should come home when the little waiters ate their lunch.

She would rather have stayed and helped at home, but having a strong suspicion that she would be somewhat in the way, she went off very pleasantly, and the cooking party set to work in good earnest.

" Now for our new recipe," said Aunt Jane.

No. 169—STEWED SWEETBREADS.

Lay the sweetbreads in milkwarm water for an hour, having first carefully trimmed off all bits of skin and fat. Then throw into boiling water and boil hard ten minutes, after which cool them off in ice-water until they become white and firm. Then stew until tender in a very little water, add for each one a heaping teaspoonful of butter, a little chopped parsley with pepper and salt, and a little cream, together with the yolk of a hard boiled egg rubbed to a powder. Let them simmer in this gravy for five minutes; then send to table in a covered dish.

" The sweetbreads will require three-quarters of an hour to stew," said Aunt Jane, " so we will begin on them

13

about eleven o'clock, as our lunch is to be at one. They
are something you can't hurry. Next come our two
ways of cooking potatoes."

No. 170—Potato Croquettes.

To every cupful of mashed potato allow a tablespoonful of melted butter, and beat to a cream, seasoning
with pepper and salt. Beat up two or three eggs, according to the quantity used, and add this to the potato, with
some minced parsley. Roll into oval balls, dip first in
beaten egg, then in bread crumbs, and fry in hot lard.

No. 171—Potato Ribbon.

Choose the largest and soundest potatoes you can get
for this dish; pare them and lay in ice-water for an hour.
Then pare off a small continuous strip, round and round,
with a small, sharp knife, or an instrument which comes
the purpose. Handle with care and fry a few at a time,
in deep lard; then arrange neatly upon a hot flat dish.

"Oh, what a funny-looking thing that must be!" cried
Rose. "Can we do it to-day?"

"I'm afraid not. The potatoes are rather new yet for
this purpose, and we should only waste our time, but in

the winter it would be quite a curious experiment to see how well you could do it. And in the mean time, perhaps your mother will get a parer for you."

" Shan't we need something else beside peach pie for dessert, Aunt Jane?" said Grace.

" I was thinking of a chocolate meringue," replied her aunt, such as you have a receipt for, No. 111. I think you might set about that immediately, and then it will have time to get cold. When it is done, you may make up the potato croquettes, and get ready the egg and bread-crumbs to fry them in. They won't suffer by standing two or three hours. Amy, you may take this delicate young cabbage that I found in market yesterday, and slice it with the cutter into fine shreds; then make this dressing for it."

No. 172—COLDSLAW DRESSING.

Beat two eggs in a bowl that fits in the top of a tea-kettle; add a gill of vinegar and water mixed, an ounce of butter, an even teaspoonful of salt and one of sugar; place the bowl over boiling water and when hot stir until it is thicker than boiled custard; then strain, and leave it until perfectly cold before pouring over the coldslaw.

When the dish is served, sprinkle a little black pepper over the top.

"Rose, you may make some baking-powder biscuit for us, to be ready fully half an hour before lunch—we don't want them hot. And now I'm going to try an entirely new receipt, one that I cut from a newspaper, telling how to make such coffee as they have at the 'Vienna Bakery.' I don't know anything about it, but I think from its looks it must be good, and it will be a novelty to our friends, I am sure."

No. 173—VIENNA BAKERY COFFEE.

Make coffee in the ordinary way; then to one pint of cream heated over boiling water allow the white of an egg beaten to a froth; add three tablespoonfuls of cold milk to the egg and mix it well, then remove the cream, when hot, from the fire, and add the egg, stirring briskly for a few moments. Serve the coffee in the usual manner, adding this mixture instead of cold cream.

When all had been accomplished that the girls had started on, they proceeded to set the lunch table, under Aunt Jane's direction. She showed them how necessary to symmetry it was to have every place, or "cover," as it

is called, abroad, set exactly opposite another, and how
the double supply of knives, forks and spoons must be
made into a square around each napkin. A dish of fruit
stood in the center of the table, with a lovely arrangement of flowers on each side of it, and some of the dishes
and various relishes were also set on, but the most important of the instructions related to the manner of serving.

"There musn't be any rattling and clattering of spoons
and dishes when you are changing plates. Each plate
that is to be used for pie must have a place by itself with
a saucer on it for the meringue; then when you have removed the first set of plates, which must be done as quietly as possible, you must take one plate and saucer in each
hand and set them before two guests; then go back to the
table for two more. You will not need extra knives and
forks and spoons, because all these are put on at first by
each plate. Then for the fruit you must lay a doyley on
each fruit plate, set the finger bowl on it, and carry them
round in the same way. As it is probable that only forks
will be used for the pie, the knives will remain on the
table ready for the fruit; but you must look at each place,
and if you see one without a knife, lay one down quietly
at the right hand when you put on the finger glass."

"Oughtn't the salad to be served as a separate course, Aunt Jane?" asked Grace.

"For formal company it ought; but these are all friends who won't expect so much ceremony, and I think three sets of plates are enough for you little girls to handle. You must all move about as quietly as possible, and be especially careful not to run against each other while you are going around the room. When your mother is pouring the coffee, wait until she has two cups ready, then take one in each hand. Remove the plates in the same way, as soon as you see any two that are entirely done with. Have your eyes wide open to see when any one of the guests is in want of bread, or butter, or any other thing that ought to be handed, but be careful not to offer the same thing again to a person who has refused it once."

"How can we tell, Aunt Jane?" said Grace.

"You yourself may take entire charge of the bread and biscuit, and Amy of the butter and pickles; then you'll be able to remember. It is a great plague to have to say, 'No, I thank you,' over a dozen times while one is trying to talk to one's neighbor. Of course you don't need to be told that when you offer any thing which you keep in your own hand, it should be done at the left hand of the guest; when you set down any thing, like a cup or plate, it must always be done from the right hand."

"I see why you should pass a thing at the left side, Aunt Jane," said Rose, "but I don't see why you shouldn't always do it from the same side."

"Because when you are setting down anything before a person seated at the table, it is apt to bring your elbow inconveniently near her, unless you are constantly on the watch to prevent it, and it is much simpler to set things down always from the other side. You'll find it so as soon as you begin to do it."

Many more were the particulars into which this good aunt entered with her attentive and zealous little pupils, but we have not time to detail them now. We must go back to the kitchen, where the final cooking was still to be done.

"Now the sweet-breads are ready for their last immersion, Grace. Just follow the directions and you can't miss doing them well. The croquettes will go over in about fifteen minutes, and the lard must be 'hissing hot' to be ready for them. Amy, you may take a large knife and fork and cut up the coldslaw a little, before you pour over the dressing. It is very unmanageable when it is in

such long strips. Mix the dressing with it thoroughly
in that common dish, before you lay it on the one it is to
come to table in; we will use a flat dish and put a border
of sliced tomatoes round the edge. Don't forget the
pepper over the top. Rose, you will want a flat dish for
your croquettes, not a covered one. Lay one row down
first in neat order, then put another on it with one or two
fewer croquettes; and so on, until there is only room for
one at the top. It is just as easy to make things look
pretty and attractive as commonplace."

The Vienna coffee was the only thing about which Aunt
Jane had not felt perfect confidence; but she followed the
directions, or rather Amy did so under her supervision,
and the result was very gratifying. The amateur waiters
carried out their instructions in a way that showed what
close attention they had paid to them, and at the close of
the repast, being joined by Mabel and Jessie, who had
been prowling about for some time awaiting the auspi-
cious moment, they all sat down together and ate their
luncheon with capital appetites.

FOURTEENTH DAY.

"Don't you think it's about time for us to cook another breakfast, Aunt Jane?" asked Grace. "We want to have some different things this time; none of the same except the coffee."

"I'm willing," answered her aunt. "We'll do it to-morrow if you like; and in the mean time I must give you some breakfast recipes. Here is one of the oldest, easiest and most respectable."

No. 174—CORNED BEEF HASH.

Take tender boiled corned beef, entirely free from fat or gristle, chop it fine, and mix with it chopped boiled pota-toes in the proportion of one cup of beef to three of pota-toes. Add enough salt to season the potatoes, pepper to your taste, mix very thoroughly together and let it stand over night. Half an hour before the time to serve, place it on the fire in an iron frying pan, with one tablespoon-ful of cold water and a teaspoonful of butter to each cup of the mixture. Let this cook slowly on the back of the stove, stirring frequently; if it becomes too dry, add boiling water. Taste it, and if not sufficiently seasoned, throw in more pepper and salt, but very cautiously. Serve very hot.

"Why, that receipt's long enough for a mince pie, Aunt Jane," said Grace.

"You'll find that following it carefully makes all the difference between good hash and poor, uneatable stuff," answered her aunt. "When hash is tossed together in a hurry it isn't the same thing as this."

No. 175—POTATOES *a la Maitre D' Hotel.*

Cut cold boiled potatoes into irregular slices, not large, and heat in a saucepan with a little milk and butter, pepper, salt and some chopped parsley. Place it over a hot fire, stirring all the time until ready to serve. To make a French dish of this, stir in half the juice of a lemon or a teaspoonful of sharp vinegar.

No. 176—POTATO PUFF.

Take two cupfuls cold mashed potato and stir into it two tablespoonfuls melted butter, beating to a light cream.

When this is done, add to it two eggs beaten very light and a teacupful cream or milk, with salt to taste. Beat again and bake in a quick oven until browned.

"We made the croquettes for lunch, you remember," said Aunt Jane, "and the puff is very hard on your little arms, for it is nothing without a great deal of beating; so we'll be contented this time with *maitre d'hotel*."

"What does that mean, Aunty?"

"A maitre d'hotel is the chief steward of a hotel or restaurant, or, in very elegant establishments, of a private family, and as he often combines a knowledge of cookery with his other accomplishments, it was natural to name a dish after him. In case you should ever want to cook a winter breakfast, I'll tell you a way to do codfish."

No. 177—Tossed-up Codfish.

Pick to pieces cold boiled codfish, or use the desiccated, which is already prepared. Prepare half a pint of thin drawn-butter, to which add half a pint sweet milk, three hard-boiled eggs cut up fine, a tablespoonful of butter, a few grains red pepper and some chopped parsley. Heat this till nearly boiling, then throw in the fish and boil up once, after which serve in a deep dish on buttered toast. It must be hot.

No. 178—DRAWN BUTTER.

Two teaspoonfuls flour and one tablespoonful butter, rubbed smoothly together, one teacupful water or milk added slowly. Boil one minute, stirring all the time to prevent its getting lumpy.

No. 179—SOUTH-SIDE OMELETTE.

One pint bread-crumbs, a large handful chopped parsley, a slice of onion minced fine, a teaspoonful of dried sweet marjoram. Beat two eggs very light, add a teacup of milk, pepper and salt to taste, and a heaping tablespoonful butter. Mix well together, and bake in a rather slow oven until lightly browned. It must be baked in a buttered dish, and turned out on a platter to serve. Do not send it to table until the family are sitting down, as it must be eaten hot.

No. 180—MILK OMELETTE.

Take a tablespoonful of milk for each egg used, beat the eggs separately, very light, add butter and salt to taste, mix all together, turn into a buttered skillet and stir constantly until done, which will be in a very few minutes.

No. 181—OMELETTE, *aux fines herbes.*

Make according to the above recipe, but before turning into the frying-pan add two tablespoonfuls chopped parsley, green thyme and sweet majoram, mixed together with pepper and salt. Put a good lump of butter into the frying-pan, and when hot turn in the omelette and fry to a light brown. To make a ham omelette of this: take half the amount of herbs and two tablespoonfuls finely chopped ham.

No. 182—CHARLOTTE MUFFINS.

One quart flour, three eggs, beaten separately and very stiff, three cups sour milk and a small teaspoonful soda, a little salt. Beat hard, and bake in muffin rings on a griddle.

No. 183—RICE MUFFINS.

One cup cold boiled rice, one pint flour, two eggs, one tablespoonful butter, one teaspoonful salt, one quart milk, or enough to make a thin batter. Beat hard and bake quickly.

"Now I think," said Mrs. King, "that we ought to be able to get a good breakfast out of all these recipes. You

may each choose one dish, and then I'll make out th
of the bill of fare."

"I don't want codfish," said Mabel.

"And I'm tired of corned beef hash," added Gra

"I didn't ask you what you didn't want, young
but what you did! Are there any of these recipe
would like to try?"

"Rice muffins," answered Grace.

"Ham omelette," said Mabel.

"I'd like those French potatoes," said Amy; "
that have parsley in them, and a great deal of white s

"All those things are nice," replied her mother,
would be enough if there were none but ladies to bre
on them, but I think your uncle will expect some
more hearty. We must see what Rhoda has in th
of cold meat."

Rhoda had some roast mutton from the day befor
some gravy with it. "Ah, that is capital," excl
Aunt Jane. "Now we can make a dish fit for a
You may write down

No. 184—MUTTON *Rechauffe*.

Take mutton gravy sufficient to cover the meat,
should be cut in small slices. If you have not e

gravy, add butter, hot water and any kind of catsup, tomato being the nicest. Add pepper or a teaspoonful of
Worcestershire sauce, a tablespoonful of currant jelly and
a little salt. Heat this nearly to boiling, then put in the
meat and let it remain just long enough to make it also
boiling hot. Having been once cooked it is better not to
cook it again unless it was under-done at first, in which
case it may simmer a few minutes longer. Serve in a
covered dish, that it may be eaten hot.

" I should think we ought to know by this time that
things are to be eaten hot," remarked Grace.

" It is something that can't be too often impressed on
the minds of cooks and waiters," answered Aunt Jane.
" How many good breakfasts are spoiled by being eaten
half cold! To be sure, if servants are directed to ring
the bell after the meal is on the table, and then the family
is late in coming down, then cook can't be blamed if her
dishes are spoiled. But I have one more recipe to give you
for a very favorite dish of mine."

No. 185—JUNKETS.

A cup and a half Indian meal, a handful of flour, half
a teaspoonful soda, one teaspoonful salt, boiling water to

make a thick batter. Take care that every partic]
meal is scalded. The flour may be mixed smo
little milk before being added. Fry on a griddl
good deal of lard.

"Shall we make them to-morrow?" asked

"Not if we have the rice muffins. And as Rhod
have to bake them and send them in by the]
it wouldn't be as much your dish as if you bake
yourselves, as you can the muffins. However, v
have some kind of bread besides muffins, and]
and see if I can find anything new for you. Yes
something I think we haven't had."

No. 186—BELVIDERE CAKES.

One quart flour, four eggs, one heaping tablespo
butter and one of lard, a teaspoonful salt.]
shortening and salt through the flour with the han
the eggs light, and add to them three quarters o
of cold milk; work this into the flour; if not en
make a stiff dough, add a little more milk; work
with the hands for ten minutes, roll into cakes ab
an inch thick of the size of a breakfast plate, and
a quick oven. At table these cakes must be bro]
cut.

" Here is something else that we must try some time or other. They are good for breakfast or tea."

No. 187—VIRGINIA WAFERS.

One pound flour, two tablespoonfuls butter, half a teaspoonful salt. Mix with sweet milk to a stiff dough, working thoroughly. Roll out very thin, cut into round cakes and roll these out again as thin as you can handle them. Dredge a little flour over a baking pan and lay them carefully in. Bake in a very quick oven. When first made they should be as thin as paper. They swell a little in baking.

" Is there anything we ought to get ready to-night, Aunt Jane?" asked Grace.

"Nothing that is really necessary," replied her aunt, " but we may do something to shorten the work a little to-morrow. Amy, you may cut up the potatoes and parsley, Mabel may measure out the herbs for the omelette and chop the ham very fine, and Grace may cut up the mutton. Don't put in any fat, Gracie, or at least very little. A strong taste of it is sure to make the dish disagreeable."

As there was somewhat more to do on this occasion

14

than on the previous one when they had prepared br
the young cooks condescended to allow Rhoda t(
the coffee. "We have graduated on that," th
marked. "As we've shown once that we are ab
perfectly, we'd rather give our time to new things.

Amy mixed up the belvidere cakes, which requi
longest cooking of any of the dishes, while Gra
lected the materials for the dish of mutton, and
up the rice muffins. Mabel gave her whole mind
potatoes, and Amy, after her cakes had gone ir
oven, prepared and cooked the omelette.

"The griddle *must* have the whole front of the
and both muffins and omelette must be cooked th
last thing; the others can be kept hot. If I had t
of that I should have advised a baked omelette, b
too late now. Well, Amy, we'll give you the
place we can at the back of the stove, and rememb
time."

But after all, the back place didn't turn out to
enough, so after a part of the muffins were bak
griddle was set back and the omelette took its place
the fire was best. Then the rest of the muffins we
for Rhoda to bake and send in hot, and the co
changed the kitchen for the breakfast table.

"This mutton-stew rather beats Rhoda," observed Mr. Vernon as he took his second helping, "though I've nothing to say against Rhoda, in a general way. And I don't believe there's any cook out of France can get up a better dish of potatoes than that; eh, Mabel? I always said my daughters should each have a profession, and I don't know but that we shall have to make cooks of them."

"Oh, papa," exclaimed Grace in high indignation, "if you're going to do that, I think we'd better not learn any more!"

"Oh, I'll throw in a little music and drawing and mathematics and such things, so that you can take your choice. But still, if the worst comes to the worst, you know——"

"I think 'the worst' will probably be Rhoda's being sick some time or other," said Mrs. Vernon; "and then I'm sure we shall be very glad to have our little daughters take her place."

After breakfast Mrs. King beckoned Mabel aside and asked her if she wouldn't like to make something for dessert all by herself. Of course Mabel said she would, and her aunt gave her this recipe, saying it was an old one of her own mother's.

No. 188—MOTHER'S RICE PUDDING.

One cup rice. ten cups milk; bake five hours.

"Why, Aunt Jane, that is the shortest receipt I
saw," said Mabel.

"That's all there is of it," answered her aunt,
cept that of course any cook would know that
should be a little salt added—perhaps a teaspoonful.
must wash the rice carefully to get out any specks o
in it, put it into a buttered baking-dish with the
and salt, shut the oven door and forget all about
your fire is steady and slow. If the fire is a quick
the damper has to be turned so as to shut off the
In this long, slow process of heating, the watery pa
the milk evaporates, and the rich, creamy remainde
comes so incorporated with the rice, that there is no
of butter or eggs. If you want to make it still b
throw in a cupful of raisins, not stoned, but just
fully picked over, after the pudding has been in
half an hour. You may just stir them up in it; i
do no harm."

"Any sauce with it, Aunt Jane?"

" I don't care for sauce with it myself, but you

make some hard sauce from your No. 156 recipe, in case the others should wish for it. It may be made as soon as you have set in the pudding, and then left in the ice-box until dinner-time."

"Won't you let me write down some more receipts, aunty?"

"Oh yes, a dozen of them if you want them, and the other girls can copy them into their books afterwards. I'll give you some that you can use next winter."

No. 189—Apple Charlotte.

Butter a deep pie-dish; place a layer of buttered bread (without crust), on the bottom, then a layer of thin slices of apple, pared and cored, grate a little lemon peel on them, and squeeze on a few drops of juice, then a layer of sugar—perhaps two tablespoonfuls—and one tablespoonful of water; then begin with another layer of bread and butter, and so on until the dish is full; cover the top closely with the peel of the apples, to preserve the charlotte from burning; this can be removed when the dish is served, and a little fine sugar sprinkled over the top. Will require from three-quarters of an hour to one hour in baking.

No. 190—Suet Pudding.

One cup chopped suet, one of seeded raisins, one of milk, three of flour, butter the size of an egg, grated rind of a lemon, one teaspoonful soda, spice or not, according to taste; boil in a form four hours.

No. 191—Foaming Sauce.

One cup butter beaten to a cream; add one of sugar and one wine-glass of wine; beat together thoroughly. Heat one and a half wine-glassfuls of wine by setting it in hot water, and add it to the other, but do not stir afterward. Let the whole stand in hot water until served.

No. 192—Cottage Pudding.

One cup sugar, half a cup milk, half a teaspoonful soda, one teaspoonful cream tartar, one and a half cups flour, one egg, or two if you prefer it; stir well together; bake twenty minutes. To be eaten with liquid sauce.

No. 193—Syracuse Sauce.

One cup of butter and two of sugar rubbed together to a light cream; yolks of two well-beaten eggs stirred in, then one cup hot (not boiling) wine. Whites of the

eggs to be beaten to a froth and stirred in at the last moment before serving.

No. 194—Rich Indian Pudding.

Eight tablespoonfuls meal (heaping), six eggs, one
quart milk, six oz. sugar, a quarter of a lb. butter, one
glass wine. Scald the milk and wet every particle of
the meal with it; then add the other ingredients. Bake
slowly two hours. This requires no sauce.

No. 195—Plain Indian Pudding.

Boil a quart of milk and pour it on a pint and a quarter
of corn meal; mix until every grain has been wet with
the milk; boil for ten minutes, stirring occasionally;
then add half a pint molasses, one teaspoonful ginger and
the same of salt. Bake three-quarters of an hour in a
slow oven.

No. 196—Suet Indian Pudding.

One quarter of a pound suet, chopped fine, half a
tumbler molasses, half a teaspoonful salt, one pint corn
meal, one pint boiling milk, half a pint cold milk, two
teaspoons ginger and the same of cinnamon. Put together
as in the above recipe, except that the meal is to be mixed

with the cold milk before being scalded.   Both these
dings should be eaten with sauce.

"There, Mabel, will those be enough for you?"

"Oh, yes, plenty; I just thought I'd like to write
down while I had a good chance, because I can't wri
fast as the rest can.   Now I'll go to work and make
pudding."

LAST DAY.

"Oh, Aunt Jane, must you really go next week? Can't you stay just a little longer? What shall we do without you?"

"It's very hard for me to go, Gracie, but you must remember that there are some people waiting at home who have had to do without me all summer. And then Amy must be back in time for the opening of school."

"I shall miss Amy so much!" said Mabel plaintively.

"Oh, you and Amy must write to each other and tell all your experiences, and next summer I hope your mamma will bring you both to see us."

"Don't you think it would be a good thing," said Mrs. Vernon, who came in at that moment, "to have one grand cooking frolic to close up with, and ask both the other families in? Considering what famous little cooks these girls have become, I think it would be quite exciting."

"It's an excellent idea," replied Mrs. King. "We must look over our recipes and pick out the nicest, and

try to show ourselves off to the best possible adva
I really think we can make a very creditable displa

"What do you say to the day after to-morrow?"
Mrs. Vernon. "That will give us time to get ready
out crowding, and it won't carry the children's e
ment about it over into another week."

"That will suit me as well as any time," replied
King, "and I want to collect all my 'cooking-class
afternoon to give them some additional recipes that
can try by themselves in the winter, and see how
they remember of what I have told them. I think
are pretty well grounded in the art."

Accordingly the class was called together for a g
examination and review. They thought it great fu
ranged themselves in a straight line just as they
school in spelling-class, so that they could "go u
down" when anybody missed. Then Aunt Jane
her catechism, passing on the questions to the n
order if they were not answered promptly.

"What is the first thing you must provide your
with when you are going to cook?"

"Clean hands and nails and tidy hair."

"Next?"

"Clean aprons."

"What must you have in the kitchen?"

"A good fire and plenty of hot water."

"What is the rule about dishes and other utensils?"

"To use just as few as we possibly can, and manage so as to take the same one for several things when it won't spoil the taste of what we're making."

"What ought you to do with flour?"

"Sift it, always."

"What must you do in breaking eggs?"

"Break each one into a separate saucer before you put it with the rest."

"And if you accidentally get one in that isn't fresh?"

"Throw away the whole dishful!"

"How about separating the yolks and whites?"

"Break them separate for all kinds of delicate cake, or for anything that is to be very light. But the recipes generally give you directions."

"Is there anything where it is best not to separate them?"

"Baked custards, and gingerbread, and such things."

"Rather indefinite, but no matter. When must you use 'cooking butter'?"

" Never!"

" And skim-milk?"

" Never when you can get any other."

" In making cake, what do you do first?"

" Rub the butter to a cream, and then put the s
with it, and then the yolks of the eggs (after you
beaten them.)"

" How do you generally put in white of egg?"

" Alternately with the flour, unless you have diffe
directions."

"And soda?"

" The last thing, except flour, and then you must
anything immediately and not let it stand."

" How do you prepare the soda?"

" Dissolve it in something—warm water, or someti
vinegar."

" And cream tartar or baking-powder?'

" Sift it with the flour."

" What kind of things need salt?"

" Almost everything except jelly or preserves."

" When you pour milk out of a pitcher or bowl w
it has been standing, what must you do?"

" Be careful you do not pour out any dregs or b
specks that may be at the bottom."

"When you are going to use gelatine or tapioca, what then?"

"Think of it a long time beforehand, and put it to soak."

"How do you strain jelly?"

"Pour it into a bag and then don't touch it till it has all run through."

"Suppose it won't run through?"

"Then you set it, very carefully, in a hotter place."

"How do you make pastry?"

"In a cold place, and hardly touching it with your hands."

"And when there is more than one layer of it?"

"Wet the parts that touch each other with ice-water."

"What do you do with tea-pots and coffee-pots?"

"Scald them before you begin, and empty and wash and wipe them as soon as they are done with."

"Is there anything else that you heat before using it?"

"All sorts of tins to bake cake in."

"What is your rule in regard to seasoning and flavoring?"

"Better put in too little than too much; you must keep trying it unless there is an exact quantity mentioned."

"What must you be sure to do when you are cooking for sick people?"

"Have everything ready at the time it is ordered, and be very neat and nice about serving it."

"How do you keep flour from getting lumpy?"

"By mixing it very smooth, first with a little milk or water, and afterward adding the rest to it slowly."

"When you want to put eggs into boiling milk what do you do?"

"Take the milk off the fire and pour it into the eggs, stirring them all the time."

"What is your rule for baking cake nicely?"

"Not to open the oven doors any more than you can help after the cake is in; only you must be sure not to let it burn."

"How can you keep things from burning that are on top of the stove?"

"Cook them inside another thing that has boiling water in it."

"When you are poaching eggs or boiling them in their shells, how should the water be?"

"Only simmering and not boiling violently."

"How can you keep Indian meal from having that raw taste that is so common in things made with it?"

"By scalding the meal so that no part of it is not wet with the boiling milk or water."

"How can you make pie-crust look nice and as if it had been freshly baked?"

"By heating it a little in the oven just before it is sent to table."

"I must say," said Aunt Jane when all these questions had been asked and answered, "I think you stand examination very well. I hope you won't let your knowledge rust out for want of practice. Now you know I've given you a mere sprinkling of recipes from among the thousands you might make if you had time and opportunity. Is there anything else you would like to have directions for?"

"Doughnuts," exclaimed two or three voices at once.

"Fortunately," said Aunt Jane, "I have an excellent recipe for them. When I was a little girl we did'nt know that doughnuts could be made in any other way than raised with yeast; but you can make such good ones with soda that one does'nt miss the yeast at all, and it is much less trouble."

No. 197—JENNY'S DOUGHNUTS.

Two cups sugar, four tablespoonfuls melted lard, four

eggs, one pint sour milk, one heaping teaspoonful soda and one of nutmeg; flour enough to roll out with.

"I ought to tell you also that risen bread dough with a lump of butter kneaded into it makes very nice crust for dumplings; and in my young days we used to think that plain dough made into balls about the size of an apple and boiled a long time, made the most delicious dumplings in the world when they were eaten hot with molasses."

"Don't you think, Mrs. King," said Edith, "that it seems sometimes rather a pity to spend so much time and money on things that are used up so soon, and after all don't do you any more good than plain ones?"

"If each one was cooking for herself alone I should think it a very poor business," answered Aunt Jane; "but when you think how much our social pleasure is increased by having nice things, and that when we make them we are gratifying our fathers and mothers and brothers, it doesn't seem so much like waste time. To enjoy cooking you must never think of your own satisfaction in eating what you make, but of the pleasure you are going to give others."

"I read a very funny story about a man's cooking, lately," said Rose. "I think any of us would have more sense than he did, if we *are* little girls."

"What was it, my dear?" asked her aunt.

"It was about Lord Byron and some of his friends. They had a receipt for a very rich plum-pudding and wanted to have a great treat; they were in some foreign country, I forget exactly where, and they had to teach their cook how to make this dish which he had never heard of. So after going to great trouble to get the materials, and following the directions as precisely as they possibly could, finally the pudding came to table, but it was in the form of soup; they had forgotten the bag!"

The girls laughed heartily at this, and at the thought of Lord Byron's blank face when he took off the cover and looked into the tureen. "You never gave us any receipt for plum-pudding, Aunt Jane," they said.

"Any common bread-pudding may be made as rich as you please by adding fruit almost *ad libitum*," replied she. "You can just mix in currants and raisins (well washed and well seeded always, remember), until it looks full enough. A real old-fashioned plum-pudding one seldom

15

sees now except at Christmas, but I can give you a very fine recipe for one.

No. 198—Rush Street Christmas Pudding.

One and a half pounds seeded raisins, half a pound currants, half a pound candied peel, three-quarters of a pound bread crumbs, three-quarters of a pound suet, eight eggs, one wine-glassful brandy. Mix the dry ingredients together first, very thoroughly; then add the beaten eggs, then the brandy; tie tightly in a floured cloth or press hard into a buttered mould. Boil five or six hours the day before it is to be eaten, then, if in a bag, hang it up until all the water has drained off. The next day boil for two hours longer and serve with wine sauce.

No. 199—Eve's Pudding.

One heaping cup bread crumbs, half a pound pared and chopped apples, half a pound seeded and chopped raisins, six ounces currants, six eggs, one teaspoonful nutmeg, one of allspice, one of salt, one cup sugar, one glass brandy, half a pound suet, chopped to powder.

"Here are some recipes for simple rice puddings that I don't think I have given you yet."

the butter into the flour and make into a paste with cold milk and one teaspoonful brandy.

No. 204—Sugar Candy.

Six cups of sugar, one of vinegar, one of water. One tablespoonful butter, put in at the last with one teaspoonful saleratus dissolved in hot water. Flavor to taste, and boil without stirring half an hour, or until it crisps in cold water.

No. 205—Coffee Cake.

Two cups sugar, one of butter, one of molasses, one of strong-made coffee, four of flour, one teaspoonful cloves, one nutmeg, one pound of fruit, three quarters of a teaspoonful soda, one and a third do. cream tartar, one egg.

No. 206—Cocoanut Drops.

One pound desiccated cocoanut, one pound fine sugar, the whites of three eggs beaten to a stiff froth. Add the sugar to the eggs, then the cocoanut, and bake on buttered paper.

No. 207—Soda Biscuit.

One pound flour, two ounces butter, one ounce lard, one and a half tumblerfuls sweet milk, one even teaspoon-

No. 200—Our Own Pudding.

Two teacups uncooked rice, one quart milk, two eggs, one half cup sugar, raisins if you wish.   If made with boiled rice the eggs may be left out.

No. 201—Union Park Rice Pudding.

One and a half teacups boiled rice, one half pint milk, a saltspoonful salt, one-half cup sugar, yolks of three eggs. Bake only until "set."   Beat the whites of the eggs to a froth, season with lemon, return to the oven and brown. To be eaten cold.

"Then here are a few others," said Aunt Jane, "that I picked out as being especially good, which I want to give you before we close."

No. 202—North-Side Corn Bread.

One cup meal, half a cup flour, one of sour milk, one tablespoonful melted butter, one of sugar, one teaspoonful soda, two eggs.

No. 203—Paste for Tarts.

One and a quarter pounds butter, one and a half do. flour, a quarter of a pound of granulated sugar; rub all

"I read a very funny story about a man's cooking, lately," said Rose. "I think any of us would have more sense than he did, if we *are* little girls."

"What was it, my dear?" asked her aunt.

"It was about Lord Byron and some of his friends. They had a receipt for a very rich plum-pudding and wanted to have a great treat; they were in some foreign country, I forget exactly where, and they had to teach their cook how to make this dish which he had never heard of. So after going to great trouble to get the materials, and following the directions as precisely as they possibly could, finally the pudding came to table, but it was in the form of soup; they had forgotten the bag!"

The girls laughed heartily at this, and at the thought of Lord Byron's blank face when he took off the cover and looked into the tureen. "You never gave us any receipt for plum-pudding, Aunt Jane," they said.

"Any common bread-pudding may be made as rich as you please by adding fruit almost *ad libitum*," replied she. "You can just mix in currants and raisins (well washed and well seeded always, remember), until it looks full enough. A real old-fashioned plum-pudding one seldom

15

sees now except at Christmas, but I can give you a very fine recipe for one.

No. 198—RUSH STREET CHRISTMAS PUDDING.

One and a half pounds seeded raisins, half a pound currants, half a pound candied peel, three-quarters of a pound bread crumbs, three-quarters of a pound suet, eight eggs, one wine-glassful brandy. Mix the dry ingredients together first, very thoroughly; then add the beaten eggs, then the brandy; tie tightly in a floured cloth or press hard into a buttered mould. Boil five or six hours the day before it is to be eaten, then, if in a bag, hang it up until all the water has drained off. The next day boil for two hours longer and serve with wine sauce.

No. 199—EVE'S PUDDING.

One heaping cup bread crumbs, half a pound pared and chopped apples, half a pound seeded and chopped raisins, six ounces currants, six eggs, one teaspoonful nutmeg, one of allspice, one of salt, one cup sugar, one glass brandy, half a pound suet, chopped to powder.

"Here are some recipes for simple rice puddings that I don't think I have given you yet."

ful soda, and three of cream tartar. Sift the soda and
cream tartar with the flour and mix well; rub the butter
very fine through the flour, stir in the milk, then work
lightly into shape on a floured board, roll about half an
inch thick, cut, lay in buttered pans and bake in a quick
oven. This may, for variety, be cut into strips an inch
wide and as long as the pan will allow.

"Now, girls," said Aunt Jane, "we *must* stop. It's
such fascinating work to talk over these nice recipes that
we are rather apt to let them steal away our time. This
is the day for deciding what we shall get ready for the
good-by tea-party for our three families and some other
friends that mamma Vernon is going to invite in our
honor. First, as to the drinks, we will have tea, coffee
and chocolate. Now, what is there in the way of bread
that we can give them?"

"Tea biscuit, Virginia wafers, company tea cake, Sally
Lunns, breakfast puffs," said Grace, consulting her list.

"I think we'll leave off those last two and have plenty
of the others. Now, we may as well assign to each what
she is going to make. Grace may take the biscuit and
wafers, Rose some baking-powder biscuit, and Edith the
tea cake. What sweet cake shall we have?"

"Dover cake with fruit in," cried out two or three at once, remembering the birthday.

"Then we must make it to-day, for it never ought to be eaten less than two days old. But we want something beside that rich fruit cake."

"Chocolate cake," "sponge cake," "macaroons," "jelly cake,"—these all at once and in a variety of voices.

"That's enough; don't drive me wild. Sister told me to let you ma'.e all that you possible could, so we'll try to get them all in. Everybody can help Grace with the fruit cake, Amy can make very nice sponge cake, Jessie jelly cake, Rose chocolate, and Edith macaroons."

"And what shall *I* do?" inquired Mabel.

"Make us some of the best wine jelly you ever tasted. And as the weather is very warm just now, we musn't put quite so much water to it, or it won't 'stand.'"

"What is nice to go with the jelly, Aunt Jane?"

"Soft custard or whipped cream; the cream is rather more attractive, I think. We'll see who has the most time left for it. As we want the greatest possible variety, there is one more thing that would look very pretty on the table with the jelly—chocolate meringue."

"Oh, do let's have it," exclaimed the children.

"So we will, and now I think our list of dainties is full enough. We'll make the fruit cake to-day, the others to-morrow, except the sponge, which must be made the same morning; the jelly to-morrow, and the whipped cream and meringue the next day, so as to have them nice and fresh. All kinds of biscuit and tea cake, of course, must be made the day they are eaten."

I wish I could tell you of the fun they all had in preparing this feast of good things, and the well-deserved compliments that were paid them by every one who joined in the repast. But as my efforts have been limited to giving my little readers some account of their cooking lessons, I must not transgress bounds by describing any thing outside. You can imagine for yourselves that it was a proud and happy day for the mothers and fathers of our little friends when they had such convincing proof of their children's progress as was afforded by the excellent supper prepared by them, and that the young people themselves, when they shall put in practice in future years the lessons of that happy time, will always look back with pleasure and gratification to the summer in which they were members of Aunt Jane's Cooking Class.

AFTERTHOUGHT.

I am told that prefaces are out of fashion; but as I h
something to say,—not to my readers, exactly, but to t
mothers and aunts,—I have begged permission to introduce
here. This little volume does not profess to be a complete ha
book of cookery, and many topics relating to that delightful
are left untouched. My object is only to excite such an inte
in the pursuit of it as may induce little people of ten or two
years old to make some playful attempts at a beginning, with
hope that in future years they may be inclined to follow it up
serious earnest.

A word as to the recipes, which have all been thoroughly tes
Some of them are taken from those precious old manuscript bo
which we all remember as the unfailing storehouses of g
things; others have been contributed by the kindness of frie
at whose tables I have enjoyed the dishes they represent;
for such as are due to neither of these sources, I am indel
principally to Mrs. Miller's charming work, "In the Kitche
and Marion Harland's admirable manual, entitled "Comi
Sense in the Household." With these acknowledgments, wl
my conscience will not allow me to withhold, I take
leave.

THE AUTHOI

INDEX.

PAGE.

BISCUIT, TEA-CAKES, ETC.

Baking Powder Biscuit...... 164
Graham Biscuit............ 147
Soda Biscuit.............. 228
Tea Biscuit............... 113
Belvidere Cakes........... 208
Huckleberry Cake.......... 144
Elmhurst Johnny Cake...... 47
Grandma's Short Cake...... 119
Company Tea Cake......... 143
North Side Corn Bread..... 227
Junkets.................. 207
Laplanders............... 148
Indian Meal Muffins........ 147
Charlotte Muffins.......... 205
Rice Muffins.............. 205
Popovers................. 9
Graham Popovers.......... 67
Breakfast Puffs........... 67
German Puffs............. 55
Sally Lunns.............. 148
Virginia Wafers........... 109
Barby's Waffles........... 151
Buffalo Waffles........... 150
Geneva Waffles........... 151

PAGE.

BREAKFAST DISHES.

Tossed-up Codfish.......... 203
Drawn Butter.............. 204
Corned Beef Hash......... 201
Veal Hash................ 46
Mutton Rechauffe......... 206
Omelette Aux fines herbes.... 205
Milk Omelette............. 204
Plain Omelette............ 47
South Side Omelette........ 204
Lexington Avenue Potatoes.. 47
Maitre D'Hotel Potatoes..... 202
Potato Puffs.............. 202

Chocolate................ 62
Cocoa Shells............. 103
Coffee.................. 49
Vienna Bakery Coffee....... 173
Tea.................... 105

CAKE.

Aurora Cake.............. 152
Bread Cake.............. 146
Cheese Cake............. 156
Chocolate Cake........... 23

PAGE.

Chocolate Cake No. 2...... 70
Cocoanut Wafers.......... 181
Coffee Cake............... 205
Corn Starch Cake.......... 138
Cream Cake............... 70
Daisy's Cake.............. 31
Dover Cake............... 55
Drop Cake................ 68
Emily's Cake............. 137
French Cake.............. 111
Henry Clay Cake.......... 55
Honey Cake............... 159
Jelly Cake................ 68
Lemon Cake............... 55
Loaf Cake................ 111
Martha's Cake............ 190
Molasses Cake............ 166
Number Cake............. 71
Nut Cake................. 145
Orange Cake.............. 70
Poor Man's Cake.......... 57
Pound Cake.............. 143
Puff Cake................ 190
Sponge Cake............. 24
Mock Sponge Cake........ 25
Ne Plus Ultra Sponge Cake.. 136
Small Sponge Cakes....... 179
Sugar Cakes............. 138
Susan's Cake............. 9
Tipsy Cake.............. 25
Tudor Cake.............. 56
Washington Cake......... 144

Bridget's Cookies.........
Crisp Cookies............
Ellen's Cookie's.........
Mother's Cookies.........
Plain Cookies...........
Doughnuts..............
Fruit Gingerbread.......
Plain Gingerbread.......
Sponge Gingerbread......
Gingerbread Nuts.......
Ginger Snaps...........
Lemon Jumbles.........
Plain Jumbles...........
Ring Jumbles...........
Macaroons.............

Chocolate Icing..........
Orange Icing...........
White Icing...........

CONFECTIONERY.

Butter Scotch Candy......
Cream Candy............
Chocolate and Cream Candy
Molasses Candy.........
Morrisville Candy........
Soft Candy.............
Sugar Candy............
Chicago Caramels........
Chocolate Caramels......
Maple Chocolate Balls.....

PAGE.

Chocolate Creams........... 42
Cocoanut Drops............. 39
Sugar Drops................ 183
Everton Taffy.............. 40

CUSTARDS, JELLIES, ETC.

Blanc Mange............... 130
Chocolate Blanc Mange..... 132
Corn Starch Blanc Mange... 132
Farina Blanc Mange........ 121
Rice Blanc Mange.......... 97
Tapioca Blanc Mange....... 133
A Good Cream.............. 158
Chocolate Cream........... 133
Whipped Cream............ 179
Baked Custard............. 9
Boiled Custard............ 24
Soft Custard.............. 25
Orange Jelly.............. 180
Tapioca Jelly............. 98
Wine Jelly................ 22
Chocolate Meringue........ 131

LUNCH DISHES.

Chicken Croquettes........ 63
Mixed Croquettes.......... 64
Potato Croquettes......... 194
Potato Ribbon............. 194
Saratoga Potatoes......... 63
Stewed Sweetbreads........ 193
Stuffed Eggs.............. 108

PAGE.

Veal Balls................. 64
Veal Loaf.................. 110
Coldslaw Dressing.......... 195
Dresden Dressing........... 66
Mayonnaise Dressing........ 65
Simple Salad Dressing...... 118

PASTRY.

Flaky Paste................ 163
Puff Paste................. 77
Paste for Tarts............ 227
Cup Pie Crust.............. 116
Plain Pie Crust............ 78
To Glaze Pastry............ 163
Apple Pie.................. 192
Cocoanut Custard Pie....... 85
Currant Pie................ 89
Currant and Raspberry Tart.. 89
Custard Pie................ 86
Lemon Pie.................. 87
Apple Pudding.............. 85
Cocoanut Pudding........... 84
Esther's Pudding........... 84
Lemon Pudding.............. 87
Marlborough Pudding........ 86
Orange Pudding............. 86

PUDDINGS.

Dumpling Paste............. 160
Potato Paste............... 161
Suet Paste................. 161

PAGE.

Baked Apple Dumpling..... 162
Peach Dumpling........... 165
Roller Dumpling.......... 160
Apple Charlotte.......... 213
Berry Pudding............ 31
Bread Pudding............ 135
Bread and Butter Pudding.. 135
Cherry Pudding........... 31
Cottage Pudding.......... 215
Eve's Pudding............ 226
Plain Indian Pudding...... 215
Rich Indian Pudding....... 215
Suet Indian Pudding....... 215
Jenny Lind's Pudding...... 141
Minute Pudding........... 140
Mother's Rice Pudding..... 212
Our Own Pudding.......... 226
Queen of Puddings........ 134
Rush St. Christmas Pudding 226
Suet Pudding............. 214
Tip Top Pudding.......... 134
Union Park Pudding....... 227

Creamy Sauce............. 31
Foaming Sauce............ 214
French Sauce............. 169

Fruit-Pudding Sauce.....
Hard Sauce............
Jelly Sauce.............
Lemon Sauce...........
Syracuse Sauce.........

SICK ROOM COOKE

Beef and Sago Broth.....
Chicken Broth..........
Egg Nog...............
Flaxseed Lemonade......
Arrowroot Gruel........
Indian Meal Gruel.......
Oatmeal Gruel..........
Plain Gruel............
Rice Gruel.............
Arrowroot Jelly.........
Imitation Asses' Milk....
Panada................
Beef Sandwiches........
Beefsteak Tea..........
Louisa's Beef Tea.......
Mrs. Miller's Beef Tea...
Old Fashioned Beef Tea..
Toast Water...........